GLIMMER OF HOPE

GLIMMER OF HOPE

HOW TRAGEDY SPARKED A MOVEMENT

BY THE FOUNDERS OF

MARCH FOR OUR LIVES

RAZORBILL DUTTON

Imprints of Penguin Random House LLC

Penguin.com

RAZORBILL & colophon, and Dutton and the D colophon, are registered trademarks of Penguin Random House LLC.

First published in the United States of America by Razorbill and Dutton, imprints of Penguin Random House LLC, 2018

LIBRARY OF CONGRESS CATALOGING-IN-PUBLICATION DATA IS AVAILABLE

ISBN 9781984836090

Photo credits on page 221

Printed in the United States of America

1 3 5 7 9 10 8 6 4 2

To those on the side of peace and justice.

*To those who were told they were too young
to demand a better world.*

To those we lost.

To those who have found hope.

CONTENTS

ON FEBRUARY 14, 2018, Marjory Stoneman Douglas High School in Parkland, Florida, was the site of one of the worst mass shootings in American history, in which seventeen students and teachers were killed and seventeen more were injured.

At 2:21, the shooter entered building 1200, known to students as the freshman building. The shooting lasted six minutes. He was apprehended a few hours later.

Instead of dwelling on the pain and tragedy of that fateful day, a group of inspiring young students channeled their feelings of hurt, rage, and sorrow into action, and went on to create one of the largest youth-led movements in global history. Their march on Washington, DC, attracted almost a million people and inspired more than eight hundred marches around the world. Today, they're leading a youth voter registration and engagement campaign called Road to Change.

This is their story.

CONTRIBUTOR NAMES AND CLASSES

Adam Alhanti, class of 2019

Dylan Baierlein, class of 2017

John Barnitt, class of 2019

Alfonso Calderon, class of 2019

Sarah Chadwick, class of 2019

Jaclyn Corin, class of 2019

Matt Deitsch, class of 2016

Ryan Deitsch, class of 2018

Sam Deitsch, class of 2021

Brendan Duff, class of 2016

Emma González, class of 2018

Chris Grady, class of 2018

David Hogg, class of 2018

Lauren Hogg, class of 2021

Cameron Kasky, class of 2019

Jammal Lemy, class of 2016

Charlie Mirsky, class of 2019, Pine Crest School

Kyrah Simon, class of 2019

Delaney Tarr, class of 2018

Bradley Thornton, class of 2016

Kevin Trejos, class of 2018

Naomi Wadler, Class of 2024, The Maret School

Sofie Whitney, class of 2018

Daniel Williams, class of 2018

Alex Wind, class of 2019

Lauren Hogg and Sam Deitsch

NOT ANOTHER NUMBER

Just another day,

Not another number.

Taking action to prevent another.

As we sit hand in hand,

We realize losing friends at school is hard to understand.

Just another day,

Not another number.

The booms in the hallways are not thunder.

Minute by minute we sit in the silence,

Wondering why we must endure this violence.

Continuously attempting to suppress our screams,

Realizing this is something we never could have imagined in
the worst of our dreams.

Just another day,

Not another number.

As we run with our hands raised above our heads we begin to
wonder,

What if not another?

We decided in that moment we could make this end,

and then maybe finally as a community, a country, a nation

we could begin to mend.

Not shocked at all, it makes perfect sense,

our country's "leaders" created this mess.

Rounds and rounds of ammunition,

register and vote to make a decision

As you make your way to the polls please don't just vote

 red or blue,

but vote for our friends who will never get the chance to.

Cameron Kasky

HOW IT ALL BEGAN: FEBRUARY 14

I do not need to tell you what happened on February 14. The tragic events that took place at my school are something far too many people know damn well. That story is one of great importance, and looking at our school system's failure to prevent this tragedy is vital in preventing future mass school shootings, but that is not the story I am here to tell. The story I can tell you in great, effective detail is one of overcoming trauma and helplessness, and mobilizing a country that has been through all of this, and failed to take action, far too many times. I am here to tell you how my friends and I ran out of school and, within hours, created and executed a plan to shine a light on just how rigged our system is and just how apathetic our politicians can be.

After evacuating school that day, I found myself on a city bus that was being used to transport students in this state of emergency. I was with the special needs students because, as the shooting occurred, I had just picked up my autistic little brother,

Holden, at the ESE (Exceptional Student Education) dismissal. On that bus, I did my best not only to text my friends and confirm that they had made it out of school alive, but also to make sure Holden was okay. As one could imagine, he hadn't truly grasped what had happened . . . though hardly anybody did, whether or not they shared Holden's optimistic and untainted view of the world.

Holden and I and the other students arrived at the Marriott Hotel right by our school, where the police began to question everyone, and we called our parents to pick us up. Holden was more confused than I've ever seen him. My phone was losing battery, the room was crowded, and we were anxiously awaiting my father's arrival. I was very glad to see some teachers and friends arrive, as I hadn't known until I saw them that they had made it. As soon as we were released, my father drove Holden and me home, and I suddenly felt a terrible feeling. I had finally realized what had happened.

When I was locked in the room at school with the special needs students, wondering whether or not I would make it out, I had three things on my mind: survival, Holden's well-being, and the fear that my friends in other classes were no longer alive. On the way to the Marriott, I only thought about my mother and having to tell her what happened, as she was out of town. It wasn't until I sat down in my father's car, knowing that my brother and at least most of my close friends—the ones who hadn't lost their phones and were able to text—were alive, that the thought came upon me: this whole time, I had been way too comfortable. Now, my reality was becoming clear. I knew that I was part of a flavor-of-the-month mass school shooting. The fact that I could easily identify this phenomenon speaks volumes for just how common this is and just how desensitized we have been to these horrific acts. As my dad, Holden, and I got closer and closer to home that night, only six words were present in my mind:

This one has to be different.

Suddenly, a dark, daunting purpose consumed me. What could I do? How could I change things? The rules are set up for Marjory Stoneman Douglas to become a part of the American School Shooting Machine. I remembered the usual narrative: Small town. Good, humble people. Some lone wolf shoots up the school. He is a misunderstood, socially ostracized kid. It was a mental health thing. Somehow, mental health shot up a school. Another a young, white male. Soon enough, the shooter becomes famous and is the hot new celebrity for the news channels to flash up on their screens.

The people of our country, while deeply hurt and truly affected, will eat it up. Flowers will be sent, cards will be written to the students ("Sorry your school got shot up!"), and thoughts and prayers will be tossed around like a common cold at a state college. Then the flowers will wilt, the people in the school and in the town will try to begin to heal, and somewhere, another school will be shot up. Maybe in a few weeks, maybe in a few months if we're lucky. Maybe a church next time. Or a concert or movie theater. It would happen somewhere, and the thoughts and prayers would, once again, mean less than nothing.

It happens so often that the entire cycle has become routine. Our shooter certainly knew what would come next: he made videos before he completed this atrocious act, where he said that everyone would know his name. To a degree, he was right. There are fan pages for him on the internet. America has a recurring illness that the media and politicians are reluctant to cure.

Arriving at my dad's house, which is about thirty minutes away from Parkland, I was greeted by my family members, who had gathered there to offer their greatest condolences and nothing but support. I didn't have much to say. I left the house, making sure Holden was calm, and went for a walk. I listened to music that was perhaps too intense and emotional. In retrospect, I probably should have just tried to calm down . . . but dammit, I couldn't. People were dead. I wasn't sure how many, but people were dead.

I crossed the lamp-lit street and began to walk over a nearby bridge. I stood and looked over the water. Nothing felt real. For just a second, everything was perfectly and terrifyingly peaceful. I believe that was the night that almost everything about the person I was before the shooting perished and fell by the wayside. Standing up there, I was reborn with an urgent, painful drive that would now determine the course of my life. I had to skip the healing process and jump right into the fight. I told myself that if the story was going to be different this time, if our school's shooting would be more than a statistic and actually serve as the catalyst, I had to get in front of cameras early on and make this message clear:

This is not the media's narrative. This is not your story. This is nobody's tragedy to interpret but our own. The students of Stoneman Douglas know exactly what happened at Stoneman Douglas, and under no circumstances will you tell our story for us.

Sometime that night, I saw a notification on my phone that a geography teacher in his mid-thirties was killed protecting the students in his classroom. A man who was my camp counselor when I was seven and my fifth-grade teacher, who coincidentally managed to also come to Stoneman Douglas— Scott Beigel. Somebody I knew and loved was murdered. I had to do this for him along with everyone else who was lost. We still weren't sure how many victims there were. I had lost people that I loved before, but it was almost always to natural causes. I had never seen something so disgusting and unreal hit me so close to home. I had always believed it never could. My whole life, Scott Beigel had been a beacon of love and humor, and now he was gone not because of old age or some sort of sickness but because somebody had shot him while he was trying to protect students. Losing Scott was what made this so much more real for me. I knew Scott; I knew his face, voice, and laugh. I would never get those things back.

After my walk, I returned to my room and got on Facebook. I saw that there was already a community event scheduled in

Parkland the next morning. I wrote two long essays on Facebook about what had happened. They went what one might dare to call viral, and suddenly, journalists followed up and were coming right to me. All of this, of course, mere hours after the mass murder in the hallways I had been walking for three years. I knew I had to speak up and get out immediately, but this new reality was hitting me hard. I didn't want to become a talking head, a broken record on every news show, but I needed the world to look at these terrible tragedies with a new perspective. I grew up consuming political media like it was candy. I was a rebel without a cause my whole life and, as a drama student, I knew how to clearly express myself. When people called us "crisis actors," they were almost right; I was an actor in a crisis. My whole life, I had been quick to speak up. Quick to be a cynic. I was always able to put my emotions aside and realize what was at stake. At around four thirty a.m., I passed out for three hours, knowing that I would be waking up bright and early. There was an event in Parkland for the people recovering, and I couldn't miss it. Our community was hurt, but we came together so quickly, and that speaks volumes about the amazing people in Parkland.

The next morning, more names of victims started to appear. I had no idea what to do or say. My mind was numb, and I had to focus. In the days following the shooting, I was on the news, again and again and again. The means by which different outlets contacted me varied. I can tell you that it was mostly through social media. For example, I was contacted by CNN to write an op-ed piece early in the day. I had to change the narrative as quickly as possible and let the country know that our generation—the school shooting generation—wasn't going to stand for this anymore. My sole focus was working to break the pattern. I immediately started writing, I started learning everything I could about gun reform, and I haven't stopped. Everything I do now is about building this movement and creating real change.

Stoneman Douglas isn't going to become the new Sandy Hook or Columbine (or Aurora, or Virginia Tech, or Santa Fe, or Las Vegas, or Pulse). A place you mention in a room and everyone sighs and says how sorry they are or what a tragedy it is. If Las Vegas wasn't enough, if Sandy Hook wasn't enough, we are going to be enough. We are going to be the catalyst for real change. This is going to count.

On February 16, two days after the shooting, a group of us, Brendan Duff, Kaylyn Pipitone, Jaclyn Corin, Alex Wind, and Sofie Whitney, gathered at my house. Earlier that day, I had done Anderson Cooper's show, one amongst many, many others. At the crack of dawn, I ran into my old friend David Hogg under the freeway that is right next to my school. I wasn't the least bit surprised to see David springing into action, as he had always been politically charged and involved. I wouldn't see David again until the next day. All I had to begin my work was my closest friends. I texted them as soon as I knew they could get involved. Jackie was already planning a trip to Tallahassee to speak with legislators and encourage them to take immediate action. In a night of brainstorming on the sixteenth, we decided we needed to march. So many great things that have happened in this country have come from displays of young people making their voices heard. This all came from a place of helplessness. It was in overcoming that helplessness that we found our strength, and we want to provide our country with the opportunity to not be helpless as well. In those two short days, we were already starting to see the cycle change. It wasn't just talking heads on the news anymore, it was me and my friends. They gave us a platform, after only twenty-four hours of real, focused effort, and we took it and ran with it. The march was about seeing how far we could go and whether or not we could truly activate the people in this country. Public displays are important, peaceful protest is patriotic, and uniting people is a beautiful thing, but real change in this country comes from the polls. It was time to destroy the apathy toward political involvement that is running our country into the ground.

People say that we shed light on America's gun violence problem, that we exposed how bad things really are. We didn't do that. America knew damn well how bad our gun problem was. We reminded America how rigged the system is. We reminded people what the NRA is doing and what Citizens United is doing to our political system. We reminded them by asking our politicians directly, in public, about campaign donations from the NRA. When I spoke with Senator Marco Rubio at the CNN Town Hall, I wasn't asking him to change his views on guns—I asked him if he would stop taking money from the NRA. When you remind American people where the money is coming from, you expose what a politician's real interests are.

We knew that seventeen of the finest human beings in the world were no longer alive, and everybody who knew and loved them would have to find a way to keep going. A gargantuan storm was coming our way, and as our group began to expand, first with more and more people showing up in my home, and later growing way beyond Parkland, we survived thanks to each other. Every day, especially as we visited the memorials and attended the funerals, it got harder. Every day, the pain got worse. But this movement and this purpose we had found kept us going, beyond what I could have ever imagined. From a movement that started with just a few friends in my living room it has become a force that could change our country. I had no idea just how large this movement would become, but knowing the power and strength of our group, I'm not surprised.

Sofie Whitney and Brendan Duff

BECOMING A TEAM: FEBRUARY 15 AND 16

IN THE DAYS FOLLOWING the shooting, the students and alumni of Marjory Stoneman Douglas High School established a home base at Cameron Kasky's house, where Brendan Duff and Sofie Whitney helped launch the social media-driven movement that would become March for Our Lives.

BRENDAN: I graduated from Stoneman Douglas in 2016, and now attend Elon University in North Carolina, which is a solid twelve-hour drive away from Parkland. So when everything on the fourteenth was unfolding around two thirty, I was watching the news from multiple states away. My little brother was a freshman at MSD, and I knew that he had several classes and friends in the freshman building. Of course, I feared the worst. I was a mess the rest of the day as the count of familiar names and faces grew. Luckily, I was with a close friend at Elon who also went to Marjory Stoneman Douglas, so she was there to empathize and grieve with me.

The next morning I spoke with my mom, who urged me to come home. I was grateful to hear her say that: I'd already made up in my mind that I wanted to come home, but I needed that push from her. I could tell by the sound of her voice that she, a substitute teacher for the school district, was devastated but still trying to stay strong. She had lost many former students just the day before.

At that point, no major coverage had taken place. Cameron Kasky, a longtime best friend who also implored me to make the trip down, told me about an op-ed he was writing for CNN, but that was about all. So I was mainly coming down to be with my friends and family and offer whatever I possibly could to console them. I began the trek on the afternoon of February 15.

That night, with only two hours to go, I got a flat tire and had to stay with my friend Bradley—another MSD alumnus—at the University of Central Florida. Initially, Bradley wasn't even planning on coming to Parkland. Both of us felt somewhat useless and detached from the situation, yet all too close and connected at the same time. I convinced him that the absolute least we could do was be a support system and hug our friends and family. The next morning I had my tire replaced and we were back on the road. Bradley and I arrived in Parkland at noon or one p.m. on the day of the sixteenth.

It was pretty hectic after that. Cameron told me that they were picking up media coverage, and people were contacting him from all over through social media. I remember him being really overwhelmed with all of the requests for interviews in a million places at once. I told him, "I'm here solely to help you guys with whatever I can, so please give me something to do."

I'm studying strategic communications at Elon, and I've interned at a public relations firm, so I had at least a little bit of experience dealing with the media. While he was at a meeting, Cameron's phone was going off nonstop. I took a couple of calls for him, organized a schedule for the next couple of hours, and offered my transportation services. He legitimately teared up, hugged me, and said, "You're hired." After that, he started responding to media with my number and would say, "This is my friend Brendan; he's my guy, talk to him."

I quickly became the liaison between the media and Cameron. When I started out, hundreds of media inquiries were coming through just asking for Cameron. When Cameron was too busy, reporters started asking if other students were available to talk. I knew Sofie Whitney and Alex Wind, two of my other best friends from MSD, were also behind starting the #NeverAgain Twitter page, so I started referring media to them. I threw people's names out wherever I could, offering whatever was possible. We started to solidify our message here, but we just needed people to listen.

SOFIE: I was there for some other stuff that happened before, on the sixteenth. That morning I woke up and had a nice long cry, because it was only two days after the shooting and I was still feeling really raw about it. Cameron texted me in a group chat with me and a few of my friends, and said he had this media thing set up: a roundtable with Lawrence O'Donnell. I felt really iffy about whether I wanted to do it, because I wasn't sure if that was what I wanted to be doing two days after the shooting. I somehow convinced myself to go, though. I said to myself that it would be a one-time thing, so it would be fine.

It ended up going well. I wasn't really knowledgeable about specific policies at that point. I was just speaking up about how I felt. Cameron and Alfonso were already really politically minded, so they did a lot of the talking. I was nervous to speak, because it was hard to believe that this was what I was doing at that point, so soon after the shooting. I just spoke from my heart and said that if the adults wouldn't do the work, the students were going to do it. It felt powerful for us to all be on the same page and be able to use our voices and control how the world sees us.

After the roundtable, Cameron said there was another interview lined up and asked if I wanted to come along. This one would be with Nicole Hockley, one of the moms of the Sandy Hook shooting victims. Once I heard that, I immediately agreed to go, because she had shown immense strength in the face of terrible hardship; meeting her could help me do the same. Cameron and I drove his Smartcar all the way over the grass in Pine Trails Park. It was so dangerous, but we made it there. At that interview, we realized that Nicole Hockley was incredibly supportive of our movement. She told us how she mobilized after her son Dylan's death. I think it was a big inspiration to us, because she felt hope from us. That was kind of crazy, because it had only been two days, and we hadn't thought about the long-term effect of what we were doing, or how it would affect other people. Hearing her say that she failed with her efforts and that she wants to be there for us, and lift us up, and support us any way she can . . . I think that was what got me to think, *This is important, this is what I want to do.* And that continued into the night, when we finished the interview and met up with some other people, including Brendan.

BRENDAN: The night of the sixteenth, Sofie, Alex, our friend Pippy, my little brother Daniel, Cameron, Alfonso, Ryan, and I were together. We went out to a Chinese restaurant and were talking about how this was turning into something way bigger than we expected. We had made a Twitter page the night before by the name of #NeverAgain. In only one night, it had gone from two hundred to three thousand Twitter followers. It was going way faster than we had dared to hope. What began as a space to spread awareness and voice our frustrations turned into something so much more. We realized that people were actually paying attention. This wasn't something that people were just sad and hopeless about: they were channeling it into us.

We definitely felt that pressure to do something with that energy, and it was a huge catalyst for the march. We knew people were looking to us for hope. They thought, these kids are speaking out for themselves and demanding that something be done—maybe they can actually make this one different. To some degree for me, but mostly for the current students at MSD, it felt like our school was shaping up to be more than something people say with hushed voices and devastated expressions. Our school was going to be a beacon of light and hope for our dejected peers.

That night we started talking about how we needed to do something concrete with this momentum. Sofie and I were managing the social media at that point, and we had hundreds of direct messages on Twitter and Facebook from people asking how they can donate and contribute, and what we were going to do next. March for Our Lives came out of that. It would be similar to the Women's March. We knew we needed help and structure, so the Women's March was kind of the model. We knew that we wanted people to be engaged—people around the country and then the world—who were reaching out.

SOFIE: People in America need a specific task or they won't do anything.

BRENDAN: Exactly. And they were reaching out with their support and kind words, but that wasn't enough on its own. They wanted something to actually do. So we gave them that direction. And that's what we hoped they would respond to.

With the announcement of the march, we were so thankful that it took off the way it did. People were starting their own marches and making it a huge national event. We watched the phone calls come in once we announced the march. Other people wanted to do more than just be there for us. That all started the night of the sixteenth.

Pretty late in the night, around ten p.m., we left the Chinese restaurant and went to Cameron's house to keep planning. I remember that we had this whiteboard, and we were crossing off different names to title the march and what to call ourselves. It was that night, when we were brainstorming names, that we invited Jackie.

SOFIE: We needed another girl in the room. There were only two of us in the room at that point, and we needed someone organized and who would actually help. At that point Jackie had already started planning the Tallahassee trip to meet with legislators, and we saw on Instagram that she was already mobilizing and getting people ready to go. Cameron was good friends with Jackie since they were little kids, so he called her up and told her about our idea for the march. Twenty minutes later she was there, at ten thirty p.m., and she's been with us ever since.

BRENDAN: We stayed really late that night; some of us actually ended up staying over. There's a picture that went around of Cameron in a Batman onesie from that night, which is pretty funny considering the caliber of the work we were doing. That night was such a motivator. I'd never met Jackie before, and suddenly there we were, giving each other orders and working on this growing national movement. She was having me call all these different senators; I was scheduling her with Anderson Cooper. It was so cool, and it immediately became this collaborative, grassroots thing. It became very clear that we needed more people and to give specific responsibilities to everyone. The whole thing blew up faster than we expected it to.

As soon as we came up with the name and the idea, the next day, media requests started coming like never before. That day I remember watching the follower count on our Twitter account grow at an exponential rate. It was all happening so fast. We really didn't expect people to listen that much at first. That's when we started scheduling the press conference for that Sunday and building our team. That process led to the press conference and the rally we held at the Fort Lauderdale courthouse.

SOFIE: All of that was happening in that few day span, when half our team didn't exist yet. Emma González wasn't part of the team yet.

BRENDAN: And neither was David Hogg. Cameron had been asked to speak at the rally that the school board had organized and that was just one minor thing planned for that Saturday. We had so much to do that day, but the rally ended up being what brought everyone together.

SOFIE: That was when our movement went viral.

BRENDAN: A lot of people were speaking: David, Emma, Delaney, and Cameron, and at that point Cameron was the only one out of the group who was with #NeverAgain. But by the end of the night, they would all come to be core members of the #NeverAgain movement, which we now humbly call "March for Our Lives." And now, we're all traveling the nation together with this group. It's amazing. Everyone stuck with it, and everyone is so passionate. It became so real that day.

Emma González

THE RALLY:
FEBRUARY 17

ON SATURDAY, FEBRUARY 17, an anti-gun rally was held at the Broward County Federal Courthouse in Fort Lauderdale, Florida. Among the student speakers was Emma González, whose chants of "We call BS" helped ignite the March for Our Lives movement.

In the days after the shooting, it was strange seeing adults not immediately scoff at our youth. For what seemed like the first time in my life, they wanted to broadcast the words of young people. They finally started to listen. And they also wanted to broadcast our words to people who had never had a reason to know or care who we were until now.

On February sixteenth, I was asked to speak at a rally by a woman on the school board of Broward County. She informed me that the rally was scheduled for the very next day, and I immediately accepted the offer. I have always best expressed myself through creative writing, so this seemed like a perfect opportunity to give a voice to the many emotions flowing through my body.

I woke up bright and early the next morning to begin writing my speech; writing until the moment I got up to the podium. (Fun fact, when I tried to print it, I found out we were out of black ink, so I printed it in blue and wrote on it from there.) This could have been my one opportunity to speak, so I gave it my all. All of my words, my thoughts, every political fact I knew; I worked hard, digging deep, within my head, and on my computer, for three straight hours. My Mom had Rachel Maddow on the TV and was saying, "Pay attention to this! It's about Chuck Grassley! You should consider putting it in your speech!" and I did. The whole speech followed a pattern: I had a thought, wrote it in a new paragraph, and in the midst of rearranging my thoughts and paragraphs, I would add on introductory sentences and fill in the gaps and delete mini rants where all I did was curse, swear, and scream in my head on the page: *"I just . . . fuck fuck fuck . . . this fucking happened. How could this have happened? So many people died, so many people died. I can't do this, I can't I can't do this . . . How do I do this? How do we do this?*

I don't remember when I found out Carmen Schentrup was dead. Carmen and I had become friends in middle school. We had science together in eighth grade. I got my period one day and didn't have a pad. I asked around and Carmen had one and gave it to me—what a Queen. We sat on the bus together after school and we would vent to each other. She would talk about her a cappella club, I would talk about my homework, and we would talk about how cool the TV shows we watched were. At her birthday parties everyone would eat pizza and watch a movie in the Schentrups' living room, and then after the movie we would all have topical discussions. We'd talk about school, and politics, and life—all good things. We'd joke about the movie we watched. I still have one of her party invitations taped up on my mirror. It was such a funny card that I put it up there immediately and never took it down.

But on the sixteenth, I found out she was dead. At least I think it was the sixteenth, when the *Herald* released the names. I'd thought she'd only been injured. I remember thinking these things very clearly; the timelines are hazy, but the thoughts are not. Neither are the facts.

Cameron called hours after I gave my speech, and asked if I wanted to join the movement that was going to be announced really soon. (I can't even remember when it was announced anymore, can't remember which night matches up to which morning.) I was told that if I wanted in, I should go with David and two media people to pick up Cameron and get dinner before another interview. I got food at the restaurant but I didn't eat it. Taking a minute to cry in the bathroom is what I did.

We worked out of Cameron's house in the early days; all of us were doing our best mentally, but we were moving so quickly that we couldn't cope in traditional ways. A lot of my friends had trouble sleeping. Even those who weren't in the building when the shooting happened had nightmares. But there wasn't much time to sleep—all of us working out of Cameron's house would have been lucky to find even a few hours, and when we did drift off, we didn't have enough energy to dream. You can see very clearly in those early televised interviews that all of us had deep dark circles under our eyes.

It was incredibly hard. Everyone had breakdowns, everyone had moments where we just needed to lie down and not do anything. But we'd still feel awful because we still felt the urgency of needing to do more. I think all twenty-five of us collectively ate two meals that entire week. No one had an appetite. No one wanted to sleep. No one wanted to leave Cameron's house to go home, even to take a shower. No one wanted to stop working. To stop working was to stop moving and think. And thinking about anything other than planning the march and the solutions for the future was to have a breakdown.

More than once I found myself crying while making phone calls in Cameron's driveway. I'd have to turn the receiver of the phone toward my ear and cover my mouth to prevent anyone on the other end from knowing I wasn't okay. The night before the press release about the March for Our Lives march I watched everyone slowly leave to go to sleep or to go home. But I didn't want to go to sleep, so I stayed. Before I knew it, it was two a.m. and I was babbling nonsense and laughing at everything, and Alfonso, the only one still there and awake, was doing a very good job of humoring me. Eventually Alfonso had to close my laptop and force me to stop working, shut off my brain, and get some sleep. Alfonso Calderon is a good and kind man.

I remember one moment from those early days particularly well. At that time, it seemed like every day someone would have a breakdown at around four p.m. That day it was Cameron, who ran off to the park in his neighborhood because he wasn't doing so hot. I followed him because I was scared he was running away from home or something. Once I saw where he was going, I relaxed enough to realize that I was having a breakdown too. Funny how that happens. He was hanging out under the bridge and I lay in the grass, looking up at the sky. I could actually feel the kinetic energy of the earth beneath me, and the adrenaline coursing through my body making me shake.

The grass was smooth and sharp and cool but the ground was warm, and the sky was spotted with clouds, so when they passed over the sun it felt too cool, and when the sun was out it felt too warm. The sun was high in the sky, though, so I couldn't really open my eyes to look at the clouds. There were trees all around and I was fully realizing, once more, how miserable we all were. How miserable I felt. How much I wished I could be a tree so I didn't have to know people who had been murdered in a mass shooting in a life I thought would be forever safe.

I willed myself so strongly to become a tree that it all just turned to tears. I couldn't stand being alive. I didn't want to kill myself—let me make that very clear right now—I just didn't want to have a human consciousness. I really wanted to be a tree.

Trees face many difficulties, what with deforestation and pollution and artificial selection, but none of that stopped me from truly wishing I were a tree.

There was so much pressure on me and so much sadness inside my tiny body. I just wanted to go back to when blood hadn't stained the walls and floors of our campus, back to when I would hang out with Carmen on the bus. Or even to hang out with my friends and not have people constantly stopping me to say, "Oh hey! You're that Emma Girl!" or "Are you from Parkland??" or "*Emma González??*"

All of us know what it feels like to be Harry Potter now. Even when people come up to us quietly to say thank you, you never know if they're someone who's going to support you or if they're just trying to shiv you or punch you or shoot you at close range, disguised by a friendly face. Going up against the country's largest gun lobby organization is obviously something that needs to be done, but our reality now is that the people we are debating and arguing against are the ones with the guns. I am personally deathly afraid of them, and I believe that they're honest in telling us the only talking they want to do is with us on the other end of their AR-15s. And people wonder why I cry a lot.

I'm a big crier, actually. I hate seeing negativity and anger and sadness and aggression, so when other people show that toward us, I am the first to admit I am a sensitive bitch, I cry often. Not all the time, but often. This is why I don't like to be negative toward people. It just makes everyone feel like shit. Sure, in the beginning we were all angry, but we were angry at people who didn't show emotion. You could go to 98 percent of all politicians and when they smile, it looks programmed. When they nod their heads, they're calculating what their response will be to shut you down instead of listening to what you have to say.

In the beginning, it was hard not to be angry. The moments that that anger abated were moments devoted to crying, and the laughs that we were able to find were few and far between. We were told in the early days of everything—I think it was week four—that we could not sustain this movement on anger alone. We needed to find joy, we needed to love one another, even the people we had previously hated. We needed to free ourselves of the negativity that was unnecessary to our daily lives, because it takes energy to hate someone, but it takes nothing to focus on what you can do to change things from being negative again. This sentiment is not to be confused with, "Happiness is a Choice." We were reminded that we were wasting energy when we could have been better using it for positive change. People with depression cannot simply chose to be happy, and I do not have depression, I am depressed—there is a difference.

I've always known that it's important to take care of myself and do what feels right to me. I shaved my head one or two weeks before I started my senior year at Douglas, but took my senior pictures before I shaved my head, so my school ID and my yearbook photo really don't look like me. People used to ask me why I shaved my head—the one main reason is because having hair felt so incredibly horrible. It was heavy, it always made me overheat in the extreme Florida temperatures, every time I put it up in a ponytail (and I looked terrible in a ponytail) it would give me a really bad headache. I was always worried that my hair looked terrible or frizzy, tangled or angled in an incorrect way; it sounds stupid but to have such a large insecurity, so prevalent in my everyday life, was often crippling. So, what do we do with insecurities? We get rid of them, cut them off at the source literally. It's liberating, a small victory to shave my head myself every week.

Everybody takes care of their mental health in their own way. Talking to therapists is a really, really wonderful thing to do, and I cannot recommend it enough. If your therapist or psychologist or whoever is helping you with maintaining your mental health isn't working out with you, you don't need to stick with that person—find someone who works for you. I take care of my mental health by communicating with the people in my life, spending time outside with the trees, listening to music, watching Netflix, drawing, painting, sewing, embroidering things (I created a majority of the patches on the jacket I wore to the march), and crying when I very much need to. Crying is really healthy and feels very good, I really don't know why people are so against it. Maybe because it's loud.

Crying is a kind of communication, and communication is key. I don't know why so many people hate communicating, because a lack of communication is what keeps us in this situation. "I don't play the politics game, I don't pay attention to politics"—well, the environment is getting poisoned, families are getting pulled apart and deported, prisons are being pushed to incarcerate more people as they get privatized and monetized, police brutality and institutionalized racism still pervade our society, rape culture might not go unchecked but certainly goes unfixed, real-life Nazis live happily among us in our everyday society, LGBTQ people are denied basic human rights and are often discriminated against to the point of suicide, millions of people live in poverty all around this country while billionaires can solve poverty for a price they would never even notice, gerrymandering manipulates our voting districts to decide the outcome of the election before the ballots are cast, Native Americans face disenfranchisement on such a level that our country is basically still colonizing them, Puerto Rico has been abandoned to the point that everyday Americans have to supply the support that the president denies them, the American education system has been turned into a business where teachers and students are piggy banks waiting to be smashed, and every day ninety-six people get shot and killed. Flint still doesn't have clean water.

You might not be a big fan of politics, but you can still participate. After all, you're not the one fighting on the floor of the House or the Senate to push legislation. All you need to do is vote for people you believe will be working on these issues, and if they don't work the way they should then it is your responsibility to write them, call them, meet with them, have town halls with them, hold them accountable—it's their fucking job to make our world better.

It's been months now, and I have times when I'm sealed up from the concept of crying. But then things start to slip. One of my friends finds an old picture or video of someone who died; another shooting happens. I hear helicopters or one too many unexplained bangs or pops in one day, and it all starts to slip. It feels like when we were at the vigil, in the hot Florida sun where Parks and Recreation people handed out water bottles to replenish what the sun and sadness had taken away. Looking for friends and finding them, hugging them, sharing tears and sweat, assuring each other that we weren't going anywhere, saying "I Love You" because we had never meant it more. Looking for friends and not finding them. Everything we've done and everything we will do is for them. It's for ourselves. It's for every person who has gone through anything similar to this, for every person who hasn't yet, for every person who never will. This isn't something we are ever going to forget about; this isn't something we are ever going to give up on.

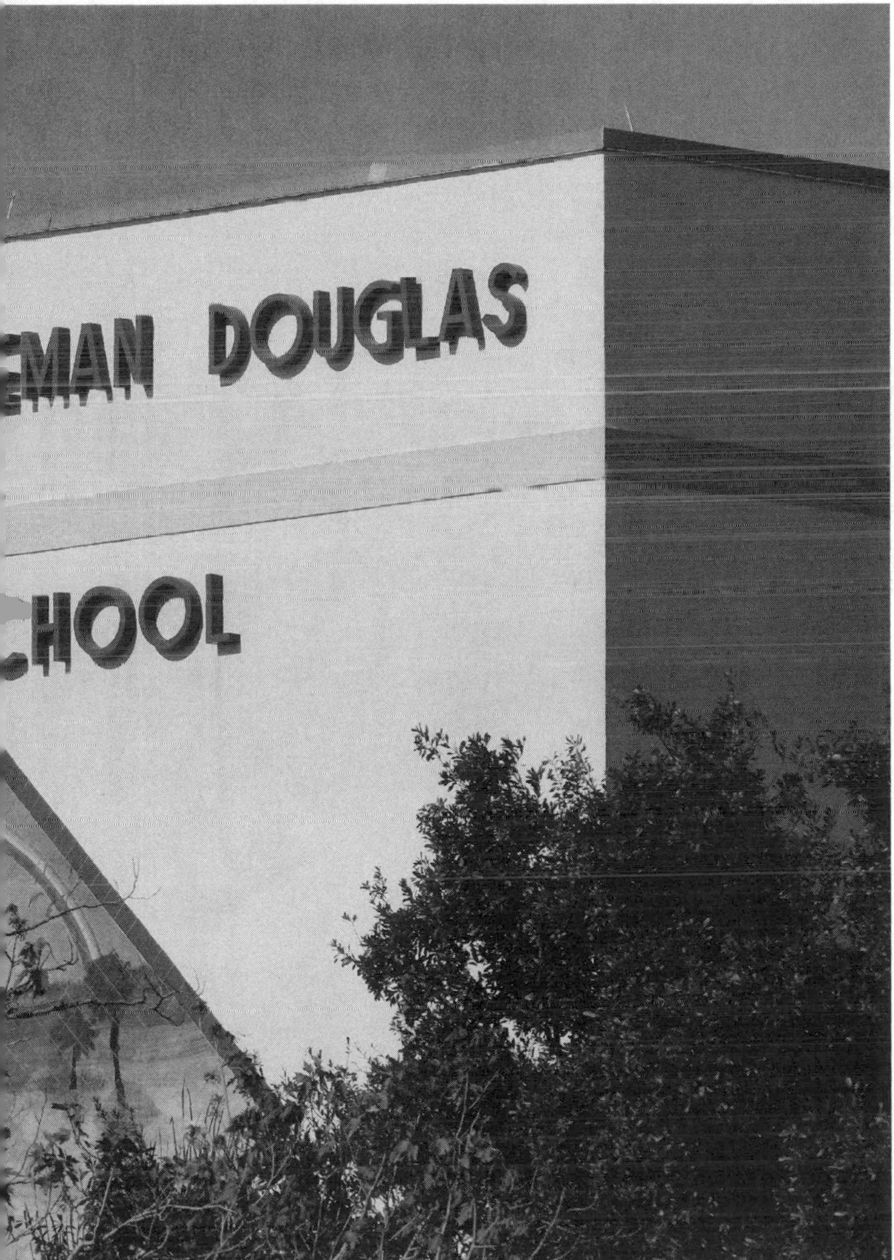
EMAN DOUGLAS
CHOOL

John Barnitt, Sarah Chadwick, & Sofie Whitney

CREATING A SOCIAL MEDIA MOVEMENT: MID TO LATE FEBRUARY

IN THE DAYS AND WEEKS following the shooting, the members of the brand-new March for Our Lives movement channeled their energy into social media, demanding policy change and direct action with the hashtag #NeverAgain. The outpouring of attention and support they garnered online gave their movement staying power, and they've learned that their generation has a powerful voice.

Our generation has grown up with new information readily available at our fingertips. Despite some of its negative effects on our culture, social media has let us access important data with ease, allowing us to be more informed than ever. And, just as importantly, the era of social media has given American youth an incredibly powerful tool: an outlet to millions of people all over the world at our fingertips.

Like most of our peers, we used to use social media for the sole purpose of procrastination, but our work for March for Our Lives has helped us understand the importance of its reach and just how effective a person's message can be when shared with people all around the world. In many ways, social media has become one of the most important tools for our organization.

But it hasn't always been this way. Tragedies like the one at our high school have been a consistent reflection of America's greatest flaws in the twenty-first century, but substantial action has not been taken by those in power, and the people of this country are confused and angry. The root of this frustrating cycle has long been a problem in America: our politicians' interest in being reelected and paid overshadows their interest in the common good of the people. This betrayal has been particularly prevalent with school shootings.

Historically, our national media has helped them get away with it. Usually once tragedy strikes, news stations come flooding in, hoping to get the inside scoop on what occurred. And in the past, news networks were the only way people could stay in touch with the world. So when past school shootings happened, people were anxious to stay informed on what new information was coming out about the shocking situation. This usually entails news channels bombarding victims that just endured a traumatic and scarring event. But slowly the media loses interest, and the nation follows their lead. Instead of fixing it or passing legislation that could prevent future tragedies, we move on to the next hot topic.

We can see how this scene played out after past school shootings. Columbine happened in 1999, before social media, only major news networks and newspapers to cover the story and inform the public. And after a while, it was inevitable that the news cameras and the nation moved on, and it became a thing of the past. Obviously people were angry and they wanted something to change, but the nationwide push for change waned when the news cameras focused on something else. After the massacre at Sandy Hook, the victims were too young and the parents were the ones who had to find the courage and voice to speak up for a change in legislation.

But the tragedy at Marjory Stoneman Douglas was in many ways the perfect storm, because we are high schoolers, we grew up using social media, and we can share what we think with the click of a button.

Our generation is so much more aware of what's going on around us than people may give us credit for. During Obama's presidency, the amount of misogyny and racism and sexism that there is in America didn't feel as noticeable. Part of that is because the first time Obama was elected, we were in elementary school and didn't know anything about politics. We didn't really pay attention to politics, because we were playing with LEGOs and Barbies. A lot of critics say, "Why didn't you do this when

Obama was president?" and "Why didn't you pay attention to these things when Obama was in office?" We were between seven and ten years old when Obama came into office. Now we're still young, but teenagers have a better handle on the world than younger kids. The older you get, the more you pay attention to what's going on around you, and the more of an impact you can have as an advocate for change.

Social media has given us the platform to say what we want to say and reach millions of people. We took advantage of that, and it kept us in people's minds because they were hearing from us directly: not from news stations, just direct information that we were putting out ourselves. That's another great thing about social media: there is no third party. In newspapers and on TV, reporters can edit what you say, and they can decide what they keep in their pieces and what they don't. But we didn't need the approval of anyone to speak our minds. We were unfiltered and unapologetic. The power for real change was in our back pockets this whole time, we just didn't realize it.

After the shooting, news trucks were lined up for miles around the school and all they wanted was a snippet of a student's story. They would bombard us, they would text us, they would tweet at us, they just wanted content and they didn't really care.

Meanwhile, we were so angry, confused, and scared, but we had a lot to say. Where does a teenager go to vent? Twitter. And because of our situation, for the first time, people cared about what we had to say. It is awful that it took such a tragedy for our voices to be heard, but now that they were being heard, we needed to use them for good. Our friend Sarah Chadwick, one of the first MSD students to go viral, describes what it was like:

> On the day of the shooting, when I got home, we didn't have any information on anything, so we didn't know the number of people who died, or the names of people who did die. More out of anger than sadness, mostly—just knowing that there was a shooting at my school—I just tweeted out. I saw Donald Trump's tweet and he offered his condolences and his thoughts and prayers, and it made me so angry. So I tweeted that we didn't want thoughts and prayers, we wanted policy and action. That was one of the first tweets that went viral. It got around 300,000 likes, and maybe around 100,000 retweets. I ended up taking it down because my dad wasn't too fond of the language I used in it. Then I tweeted out an apology that basically said, "I'm apologizing for the language I used but not my anger," and I got a decent amount of retweets and likes on that tweet, too.
>
> I had about 400 followers on Twitter before the shooting, and I think it was up to 13,000 the day after that tweet. I realized how many people were actually listening to what I was saying, so I used it to

my advantage. I tweeted that we should call AR-15s "Marco Rubios" because they're both so easy to buy, and that got a lot of attention. Laura Ingraham tweeted something like "This is how sixteen-year-olds talk to members of office." She referred to me as "sophomore Sarah Chadwick" in her tweet, so I quote tweeted it with "I'm a junior," and that tweet blew up as well.

I was known in the group as the girl with Twitter. A lot of people tell me that I have Twitter brain. I usually only speak in like 240 characters or less—I tend to have really short punchy statements when it comes to my speaking.

Before Feb. 14, my Twitter was kind of all over the place, just retweeting funny things that I saw, memes, keeping up with the pop culture of the time. I was out on Twitter before I was out to my parents, so that was where it felt the safest, and that's just where I would tweet the most bullshit basically. I made a lot of friends through Twitter. Before the shooting, I had a lot of mutuals, but I have a much bigger platform now.

By February 16, two days after the tragedy, we all realized that our social media accounts were starting to receive real attention, so we created a collective account where people from all over could contact us and share their stories. If fellow survivors or activists wanted to help us in our fight, we wanted there to be a place where we could communicate. So many people wanted to get in touch with us, and we were already making an impact. We called it @NeverAgainMSD. We struggled quite a bit about what to name it, because we had so many thoughts about what the best response to this situation would be. #NeverAgain was chosen because it really encapsulated what we wanted to get out of all of our activism: we didn't want anyone to endure the pain and hardships that Parkland had suffered.

Before the shooting, we would get maybe two retweets on an average post—social media was something we used to share memes and funny videos. But these first tweets immediately gained at least one hundred retweets. Then slowly it became hundreds of retweets and then thousands of retweets and we realized that people were actually listening.

So, our friend Daniel Williams quickly whipped up a #NeverAgain graphic and we decided that at three p.m. that day, we were going to try and get as many people to tweet it as possible, hoping that we could get it on Twitter's trending page. We posted it to support each other because at that early point it wasn't really a movement. At first it was just a group of students who were desperate to do something and make as much noise as possible before the news turned its cameras in another direction.

After a couple of hours, and a couple hundred tweets featuring that hashtag, #NeverAgain trended at number two, right under Drake's "God's Plan." I think that might have been the moment we realized the impact that our voices could have. If we could take over the internet, even briefly, with just a two-word hashtag, the distance to which our words could stretch could be infinite.

We always had a voice, but now we had an audience.

So we got straight to work. We didn't take time away to heal. This was our healing. While planning our nationwide march in less than two months, we needed to make sure that people didn't forget what happened in Parkland. That people still cared about the seventeen lives we lost at our school, and the countless lives that are lost every day due to gun violence. We have seen it with just about every shooting in this country, we saw it with Columbine, Sandy Hook, and Virginia Tech; the media will cover it for a couple days, at most, but we refused to let that happen. We were not going to allow our shooting to become just another statistic. The only way to keep people thinking about all of the senseless acts of gun violence was to keep talking about it, and not stop. So we kept tweeting and posting, grew our platforms, and never lost hope.

We got the most attention after the march because it was the day we had been working toward for a while, and during the lead-up we were all gaining a following on social media. And now, on the March for Our Lives Twitter account and on our own platforms, the people that are following us don't just want to keep hearing about our tragedy anymore. Now it's about what the next steps are, what we can do to change this. Now we don't want to tell you how angry we are, we want to shift the conversation and find solutions.

We learned all about activism through Twitter, which means we learned our activism through other teens online. It's not like there's a class at school where you go to learn about activism. Twitter and other platforms are *so* intersectional. Learning what you know from those platforms really does create intersectionality in your activism, because you can go on Twitter, and it's not just gun control that's trending, it'll be DACA, and ICE, and so many other things, so it's kind of forcing you to have intersectionality in your activism, which I think is an amazing thing. All of these issues feed into each other, and we can all learn from different movements to be effective protesters and activists.

We can't begin to say how many times old people that we meet in the street have compared the March for Our Lives movement to the Civil Rights movement and the people that protested the Vietnam War; some of the greatest changes in our history were brought up by young Americans who were sick of not having their voices heard. Even the one and only John Lewis compared us to himself, and told us to keep stirring up "good trouble," and Dr. Martin Luther King Jr.'s family has given us nothing but support. These are leaders whom we have learned about in school, people whom we emulate in so many ways. Courageous young people throughout history have yelled so loud that it turned the country upside down. Our goal is to do the same; what makes us unique is that our rally cry is heard far beyond the streets. Our rally cry is live-streamed, posted, shared, sent, retweeted, and heard all around the world in no time at all.

Our tour is our next big step, so we've used our social media accounts to publicize it, but we also use them to shine a light on other activism that has sparked from this, like the National School Walkout. We really tried as a group to amplify the organizers' voice because obviously they are doing great things. Change the Ref, an organization started by Joaquin Oliver's parents, has been doing so much, and we've been working with Joaquin's father, Manuel.

Just after the tragedy, we used social media to advocate for what we believe in. Now that we have this platform, we're using it to help other people who are advocating for what they believe in, to amplify their voices and give them an audience, because they deserve as big an audience as we do.

Our organization has extended past #NeverAgain, past Parkland. What we're fighting for is so much bigger than just us. Victims of gun violence from all over the United States, all over the world, are connecting with our message. March for Our Lives is about giving survivors the chance to use their voices, a chance they never thought they'd have. It did not even have to be just us spreading the message: people all across the country were eager to keep the conversation going, and excited about the opportunities that were now available to them. The movement that we created has given a voice to an entire new generation of people.

In the days and weeks following the shooting, well-wishers flooded the area surrounding the school grounds with flowers, stuffed animals, crosses, and other gifts to show solidarity with Parkland This fence was one area near the school that was accessible while the school remained locked down.

Lulu the three-legged greyhound was one of the many emotional support dogs brought in to comfort the students of Marjory Stoneman Douglas when they returned to school.

Seventeen angels representing the seventeen victims light up the amphitheater stage at the February 15 vigil at the Parkland Recreation and Enrichment Center.

(From left to right) *Cameron Kasky, David Hogg, Jaclyn Corin, Alex Wind, and Emma González announce the March for Our Lives at a press conference outside Marjory Stoneman Douglas High School on Sunday, February 18.*

Jaclyn Corin holds a painted stone placed by well-wishers near Marjory Stoneman Douglas High School on March 27, 2018. The stone is one of countless gifts piled in front of the school's entrance sign.

Jaclyn Corin and Alex Wind meet with students after participating in a panel on gun violence at Harvard University on March 20, 2018.

The March for Our Lives stage in the early hours of March 24, 2018, just before the demonstration began in Washington, DC.

Hundreds of thousands of people marched on Washington for the March for Our Lives, one of the largest demonstrations in US history.

Emma González and Nikhita Nookala at the March for Our Lives in Washington, DC.

Emma González and other students from Marjory Stoneman Douglas and schools around the country flooded the stage at March for Our Lives in DC.

Cameron Kasky and Emma González celebrate after the March for Our Lives in Washington, DC.

Victoria Gonzalez, the girlfriend of Parkland shooting victim Joaquin Oliver, marches on the night of June 15, 2018, on the South Side of Chicago, Illinois.

Jaclyn Corin (bottom center) with Chicago Strong leaders Mya Clark (left), D'Angelo McDade (top center), *and Kobey Lofton (right)* at the Peace March in Chicago on June 15, 2018.

Sofie Whitney holds a sign made by local students at a town hall in Milwaukee, Wisconsin, on June 23, 2018.

Tokata Iron Eyes of the Standing Rock Youth Council brings the Road to Change crew to the Standing Rock Reservation on June 27, 2018.

Students from Parkland, Houston, Santa Fe, and Chicago on the Road to Change nationwide tour sell merchandise at a stand in Albuquerque, New Mexico, to benefit local organizations on July 11, 2018.

The Road to Change tour spoke to a crowd at the California African American Museum in Los Angeles, California, on July 19, 2018.

Members of March for Our Lives meet with students from a local chapter of the Children's Defense Fund Freedom School at the University of Southern California on July 20, 2018.

Alex King, a founder of Chicago Strong, speaks at a community event in Huntington Beach, California, on July 21, 2018, as part of the Road to Change nationwide tour.

Participants hold up portraits of gun violence victims from Parkland, Florida, and Santa Fe, Texas, behind speakers at the Orange County rally on July 21, 2018.

Victoria Gonzalez stands with Joaquin's mother, Patricia, in front of a mural created by Joaquin's father, Manuel, in Sunset Park in Henderson, Nevada.

Jaclyn Corin

THE TRIP TO TALLAHASSEE: FEBRUARY 21

TUESDAY, FEBRUARY 20, MARKED the day that one hundred teens from Marjory Stoneman Douglas traveled from Parkland, Florida, to Tallahassee, Florida, for a two-day lobbying trip. Jaclyn Corin organized over seventy meetings with state representatives on both sides of the aisle to discuss sensible gun legislation in the state of Florida.

The very moment grief moves into your life, it never leaves. Grief trails behind you like a shadow, making you painfully aware of its presence at the worst of times.

My mind will never be at peace. There will always be a hole in my heart that was chewed away on Valentine's Day. My escape from Marjory Stoneman Douglas High School will always be the greatest blessing of my life, and never will I live a day where I do not think about the people who weren't as lucky as I. The beauty of life is a privilege, not a guarantee, even at seventeen years old. To my family, friends, and members of law enforcement

69

that protected and comforted me on February 14—I am forever thankful for you.

After I fled from school, my dad found me frantically running through a jungle of students and teachers. I hugged him tighter than ever, knowing some parents would not get to do the same that night. Together, we made our way back home, taking an alternate route because the main street was blocked off with ambulances, police cars, and SWAT tanks.

When I stepped inside my home for the first time, I dropped to the floor, physically and mentally exhausted. While my dog licked the tears off of my red-hot face, I stared blankly. I didn't know what to do with myself. I was lost. Should I be upset? Angry? Grateful that I'm alive? There were far too many emotions flowing through my body, and my head continued to pound from all the hysterical crying.

Eventually, I ate my first bite of food of the day: a Valentine's Day chocolate. Soon after, my mother came home—she's a teacher at the local elementary school, which had also been on lockdown. The next two hours were spent answering the incredible number of texts, missed calls, and Facebook messages from people around the world, all checking in to make sure I was safe.

It wasn't until I turned on the TV that I felt the first wave of emotion: anger. The screen displayed a chart of mass shootings throughout US history, which included Virginia Tech, Sandy Hook, Las Vegas, and Columbine. All names of shootings I was accustomed to seeing on the news, except the last one. The last row of the chart read "Marjory Stoneman Douglas High School." I did a double take; that chart did not make any sense whatsoever. I had thought the casualty count was only three at that point, but now the screen read eleven.

Eleven deaths at *my* school? No chance.

The denial only lasted for a second. I began to scream at the TV, knowing that I wouldn't get a response back. I yelled at a piercing volume, realizing that my school was a statistic, and now always will be.

A few months before, I was assigned a project in my AP Language and Composition class on gun reform. At the time, the subject didn't mean much to me, but writing the essay gave me valuable insight that I did not know would become so terribly real. I already knew the basic truth behind why and how the shooting happened. This was more than just one person's doing; I knew it was an entire system that led to the deaths of my friends.

I sat in my room at night and helplessly watched the screen, the number of casualties rising and my heart breaking into even more tiny pieces. All over social media, my classmates were posting prayers with the hashtag #DouglasStrong.

On my profile, however, I used rhetoric that resembled no one else's. I took to Instagram and Facebook and posted a picture that read "MAKE IT STOP" above a drawing of a semi-automatic rifle. My caption read ". . . contact your state and local representatives, as we must have stricter gun laws immediately.

We need to work together to bring change to this country so that something like this never happens again." In a very short period of time, my post received hundreds of shares.

The next morning I woke up with an even heavier heart. The count was now seventeen, a number that will forever haunt me from that day on.

I started to get ready to go to grief counseling at our local community center. Being with psychologists and friends seemed like the best option for me at the time. As I walked out the door, though, my family friend gave me a call. She explained that she had seen my post from the night before and wanted to connect me with a congresswoman if I was serious about mobilizing.

"Of course I'm serious. If we're going to do something it needs to be now," I explained.

Later that night at the community vigil, I met with the congresswoman. At first I was terrified to speak to her. I mean, what seventeen-year-old has to meet up with a federal government official?

According to her, there was a session in the Florida legislature ending in approximately two weeks. If I was to make a move on a state level, I needed to work with a state senator. She gave me a contact and thanked me for being brave enough to take on this responsibility.

I realized that if I wanted anything to change, I needed to develop an ambitious plan. I felt as though it was all up to me to urge the House to bring a bill to the floor regarding stricter gun laws. But I *knew* I couldn't do it alone. I needed friends with me—*a lot* of them.

That Friday morning, less than forty-eight hours after the shooting, I explained my plan to the Florida senator. I wanted to pay a lobbying visit to our state capital alongside my classmates. I stressed to her that I needed this trip to make a powerful statement: the young people were angry, and we weren't letting this shooting end up like all the others, where people forget a week later.

Keep in mind that before February 14, my life was full of typical teenage antics, just as you'd expect. Life was a routine in Parkland—everything about the town was predictable. My thoughts were purely directed toward my grades, social life, and college prep. Never in my life did I think I would involve myself in the world of politics.

On February 15, I asked other Douglas students to direct message my Instagram page (@jackiecorin) if they wished to join the trip to Tallahassee. I received an overwhelming number of requests, so I had to cap the trip at one hundred.

As I typed up a list of names that Friday night, I received a call from my good friend Cameron. I was well aware that he had been doing interviews all day, just as I had. He urged me to come over to his house and work with him on "something important."

I quickly jumped out of my bed, hopped in my car with pajamas on, and sped over to his house. I was excited that other people wanted to make a change immediately. I didn't have to lead this alone: I now had an environment that would support and help me with my work.

I was greeted by Cameron, Sofie, Brendan, Alex, and Pippy, excited to see what they were up to. Clearly they were already well at work, and they were glad to see that I was, as well.

That night, the phrase "March for Our Lives" entered my life for the very first time. We had no clue that this single idea would be the one that would change our lives forever. From that night on, we spent every waking hour on Cameron's living room floor prepping for interviews, researching policy, and contacting other organizers. Each day, more and more change-makers would join us on the rug, passion radiating from their eyes.

I spent the next few days creating the trip to Tallahassee: organizing over seventy meetings with state representatives, devising itineraries, renting buses, ordering food, formulating sleeping arrangements, and calling parents and chaperones. The process was utterly exhausting, especially because I was still in the beginning stages of grief. Distracting myself with something productive helped me heal, though, and I made it my mission to get the job done regardless of any mental or emotional setbacks.

After days of breakdowns, constant pacing, and endless phone calls, the trip was completely planned. I had barely slept or eaten. One day, I consumed nothing other than a handful of peanuts and sips of water. I'm a class president so I knew how to successfully plan events, but never had I organized anything of this caliber—no kid should *have* to.

The night before we embarked to Tallahassee was only five days after the shooting. I called a meeting at the local community center for all the kids and parents to go over the schedule and hand out consent forms, as if it was a field trip. There were so many cameras pointed at me; it was then when I realized the world was watching. Parkland was now the epicenter of the country's often-sparing attention, and we couldn't let this opportunity slip from our grip.

The next day, in the early afternoon, three coach buses sat waiting for us at a local parking lot. In truth, I was worried no one would show up, especially the press. To my surprise, every single student that signed up was there on time, many students coming straight from Carmen Schentrup's funeral. At least a dozen news trucks were in attendance as well, all of which were covering the start of what we hoped would be a monumental movement.

I climbed on top of a CNN SUV with Cameron to make announcements to the huge crowd. We screamed at the top of our lungs as we thanked everyone for being so dedicated. There was a dent atop the car afterward—the first of two cars Cameron would dent by the end of this.

After a dreadful seven-hour bus ride, we arrived in Tallahassee and were greeted by students at a local high school. I didn't expect to feel so much warmth in that moment, but it ended up being the first time I felt immense support from a community outside of Parkland. Standing in the cafeteria of the high school,

I finally got to breathe and say "I did it." I was relieved everyone got there safe and sound, and I was over the moon that my hard work was paying off.

Overnight, our large group slept at the local civic center. We cuddled in our cots on the floor, which had been supplied by the Red Cross. The rooms were filled with constant chatter—students spent all night researching talking points and solutions, making sure they were completely prepared for the next day.

In the morning, we woke up bright and early, arriving at the Capitol Building as soon as the workday began. We divided into groups of ten to fifteen to cover the most ground.

Over the course of the day, we met with countless representatives on both sides of the aisle. It's important to remember that this is a nonpartisan movement; it shouldn't be a Democratic or Republican ideology to want to save lives. We also met with the attorney general, lieutenant governor, and governor. We sat in on a Senate meeting where they sent thoughts and prayers to Parkland, but promised no action. Naturally, everybody who had found themselves in those rooms was furious that our lawmakers were so apathetic.

I had walked into the day with immense hope in my heart, but I soon realized that people only had sympathy for us—they weren't willing to *do* anything to prevent the next shooting.

There was a common thread in every meeting we took—avoiding a real conversation about guns. It was incredibly disheartening to recognize the pull that lobby groups truly have, specifically the National Rifle Association. We spoke about arming teachers in schools, most of us finding that idea absurd, considering gun violence does not *just* occur within school walls. My peers and I advocated for placing more psychologists in schools—something almost all people can agree on. Our governor proceeded to cut mental health funding after our visit.

After a day filled with meetings, a huge weight was lifted off my shoulders. We jumped back on our coach buses and rolled home, disappointed yet even more motivated than before. The trip was now over, but the movement was surely not.

The experience was definitely a reality check. Looking back, it prepared me for future encounters with politicians. The Tallahassee lobby trip was an early warning that this process would be more difficult than I had previously thought.

I fully believe that our presence there made a difference. It proved to our state government that the shooter messed with the wrong school. They surely did not expect immediate action, specifically one hundred teenagers swarming their building like bees.

The trip also served as a lesson for all the students, especially those who were unaware of how the government functioned prior to lobbying. We were exposed to a lot of carelessness by our "leaders," which pushed a lot of kids to continue using their voice when we got home.

A little over a week after our trip, the governor of Florida, Rick Scott, signed into law Senate Bill 7026, entitled the Marjory

Stoneman Douglas High School Public Safety Act. It called for a ban on bump stocks, and raised the minimum age to purchase a firearm from eighteen to twenty-one. These two initiatives were certainly progressive, but it wasn't enough.

To counterbalance the package, however, the law also includes the Coach Aaron Feis Guardian Program, which arms some teachers if both a local school district and sheriff's department agree. My county, Broward County, decided against the program, but other communities in the state now have the option to put *more* guns in their schools.

I will never stop fighting to disarm hate. I owe that much to myself, my school, and every community where gun violence is normalized. It might take years, but we must continue to move forward as a united force to bring about the change this country desperately needs.

Cameron Kasky and Chris Grady

CNN TOWN HALL: FEBRUARY 21

ON WEDNESDAY, FEBRUARY 21, CNN hosted a Town Hall that gave Marjory Stoneman Douglas students the opportunity to ask honest questions of Senators Bill Nelson and Marco Rubio, Representative Ted Deutch, and NRA spokeswoman Dana Loesch. Two students, Cameron Kasky and Chris Grady, recount their now-famous confrontation with Senator Marco Rubio about accepting contributions from the NRA and his stance on military-grade weapons.

CAMERON KASKY: On February 21, Stoneman Douglas students, parents, and teachers alike attended our famous Town Hall, hosted of course by CNN. That day, I was driving around in my father's Smartcar working on press. In case you did not know, a Smartcar is a two-seat vehicle designed by Swatch and Mercedes. The thing is tiny. My car was in the parking lot at school and therefore locked in for several days as law enforcement and administration rightfully did not want to open the premises until they had cleared everything up. As evening came closer and I knew I was attending the Town Hall, I went home and quickly threw on my purple shirt and black tie. With my vindictive rage still strong as it had been a week before, I entered the Smartcar feeling like a much less exhilarating pitch for *Knight Rider*.

Upon arriving at the Town Hall, I learned I would not be allowed onstage to ask my question. I had to push CNN very hard to let me on. It was on stage that night that I got to see Scott Beigel's parents for the first time after the shooting.

The most exciting part of the night was when Senator Rubio came onstage and I was lucky enough to shake his hand. Rubio has constantly been a pariah to pretty much everybody in politics. Trump is not a fan, the Democrats aren't fans; he is not particularly good at making friends. That being said, I have always deeply respected Rubio for his ability to speak in front of audiences that will chastise him. It's one of the main reasons I have such an immense appreciation of Bobby Kennedy. Love them or hate them, being able to speak in front of a booing crowd is no easy task. Now, mind you, I believe the two people I just mentioned are incredibly different. Kennedy had balls; Rubio is just spineless.

Nevertheless, I thanked Rubio for actually bothering to show up (Governor Rick Scott did not show up because he is running for Senate this year and knew he wouldn't make it out of that Town Hall with any voters). Rubio was wearing an awful lot of makeup. Also onstage were Senator Bill Nelson and Congressman Ted

Deutch, both of whom I had seen in the few days prior, as they had been very active and engaging in our community.

Anybody who knows our story wants me to talk about my question for Rubio, and I'd like to clarify some things: First of all, many said I was disrespectful to Rubio and completely out of my place. I'd like to make it clear that I shook the man's hand and encouraged the booing audience to allow him the opportunity to speak. I believed we should hear him out. Second of all, I asked a very simple yes-or-no question: Would he stop accepting money from the NRA? It was entirely Rubio's choice to give a politician answer, and that is how he lost that night. In a room of people sick of politicians' typical bullshit, he thought it would be a good idea to try and sidestep an incredibly simple question.

I understand why he thought he could get out of that completely clean. He had been handed softball questions the whole night leading up to me. He probably thought he was going to make it out of that with zero consequences. Unfortunately, I wasn't going to let him get away that easy. If you are a politician, you work for the people, and it is your responsibility to answer the questions the people rightfully raise. Senator Rubio should not expect easy questions. If they were easy, they would not go to the senator. His job is to make key, important decisions, and it was that night that he showed his true colors.

CHRIS GRADY: February 21 was probably one of the craziest days of my life. It's something I'll remember vividly forever. We started the day with a seven-hour drive to Tallahassee to meet with our state legislators. Jackie Corin set up the whole trip, and it was really cool. It felt like the movement was starting to gain momentum and people were paying attention, but I felt a lot of conflicting emotions that day. On the drive up, we learned that the Florida House of Representatives voted down a motion to consider new gun laws. They weren't even voting on the bill! The fact that they voted down even having a debate about the bill on the floor felt like a slap in the face on the drive up. It was rough.

I had expected it would be cool to see the inside of the House and meet with the legislators. But when we got there, even though it was exciting to be there and see it all, after that vote, the meetings felt like publicity stunts for the legislators. They treated us like we were sick puppies, and it just didn't feel like we were being taken seriously. The first person we were supposed to meet with, who was actually a Democrat, was late to the meeting. We asked his aide why he was late and the response we got was that "he's not a morning person." It pissed me off.

It wasn't like we were expecting things to happen immediately, but the fact that we knew going into those meetings that the House wouldn't even debate the bill made the meetings that morning especially frustrating. I knew it would take a lot more work to get our representatives in Tallahassee to listen to us.

We had to get home in time for the CNN Town Hall that night, so we flew back down to Sunrise, Florida. I didn't actually think I would be speaking at the Town Hall; I was going to support my friends who were. I submitted some questions a week before, but a lot of people did. When I got there though, a producer found me and handed me the question I had submitted. He told me that there was a chance I might not get to speak, but he gave it to me so I would be prepared if Jake Tapper called on me.

We went backstage and I saw one of my favorite teachers I've ever had, Mr. Levine. He taught English 2 when I had him as a sophomore, and he was a teacher I really respected, so it was cool to see him there. I felt like if I ended up having to speak, he would be there supporting me, so that helped.

I wanted to ask Senator Rubio if he thought there's a place in our society for high capacity magazines capable of firing fifteen to thirty rounds or more. I think this is a super important commonsense policy stance: Military-grade weapons shouldn't have a place in our society. If he honestly felt differently, I wanted to hear him defend it. Before the Town Hall started, I kept reading and rereading my question, and I didn't think it was enough. Maybe I was just nervous, but I wrote another paragraph on the back of the page to open up with just in case.

Really early on, Cameron actually gave me a shout out from the stage, which I didn't expect so I was kind of, I don't know, embarrassed. At the beginning of my senior year, I enlisted in the army. Prior to the tragedy I was biding my time eagerly waiting until the day I shipped off to basic training. I had dreamed about joining the army since I was a little kid. So Cameron asked me to stand up and then he asked Senator Rubio if he could promise that I'd make it through high school to get to basic training, which was pretty intense.

After Cameron pointed me out, I realized I probably would get to ask my question. It turned out I was right. A producer ran up to me and was like, okay, here's a mic, stand here, you're going to ask a question in a few minutes. That's when I got *super* nervous. When you watch the video, you can see I'm, like, just shaking in place, or I'm swaying back and forth. I couldn't stand still. Jake Tapper introduced me in the audience and told the crowd how I enlisted in the army, which meant a lot to me. And then it was my turn.

I started out by saying that even though we might not see eye to eye on everything, our representatives need to come together with your colleagues on both sides of the aisle to fix this, because children are getting killed every day. And then I asked my question. Senator Rubio's answer really surprised me. He traditionally hasn't supported putting a cap limit on magazines, but he said he's starting to change his mind on that. He said while it might not have prevented an attack, it could have saved lives, which is true, because the shooter who shot up my school was able to fire over one hundred fifty rounds in about six minutes.

After the Town Hall, we all went out for a late dinner, and at the restaurant we went to, we ended up running into a guy who turned out to be Helena Ramsay's father. Helena was one of the victims from MSD. He thanked us for everything we were doing.

I remember he said that he used to feel like he didn't really have much hope in this generation, seeing how we're always on our phones, things like that. But after all of this happened, he realized how smart and passionate we can be. He encouraged us to keep fighting and doing what we're doing. To end the day that way, with that conversation, it really put everything into perspective for me. Even if at times I felt unsure about what I was doing, or I was nervous about something, or I was exhausted from working hard, I knew that what we were doing was right, and that it meant the world to a lot of people.

We left Tallahassee feeling a little defeated, but then a few weeks later, Florida legislators raised the age limit from eighteen to twenty-one to purchase firearms, and they put more money into mental health, though there was a compromise because the bill also allowed counties to opt in to a program that would train and arm teachers. Broward County chose not to do it, and I was really proud of that. I still haven't heard anything more from Senator Rubio about high-capacity magazines though.

I learned that day that this fight was going to require a lot of effort, hope, and compromise. When I think about the twenty-first, it really feels like the movement in a nutshell, a rollercoaster with a lot of high highs and low lows. The day had its frustrations, but ultimately we had every reason to feel hopeful.

I ended up unenlisting just after the march. For now, I'm taking a gap—I don't even know, a gap semester? A gap year?—to work with the organization we've built. It was obviously a big decision for me, but I keep saying to people, how can I go overseas and protect people when they're getting shot here in their classrooms and on the streets? This is where the real fight is: home, back home. I know this movement is what's most important right now.

I do still think about it all the time, and about whether or not I made the right decision. We were in the airport in Chicago the other day returning from a Road to Change event and there were just army service members everywhere; it really hit me that I could've been one of those guys. And then out of the blue, my mom texted me this political cartoon of this guy standing in front of an army recruiter with a sign that says "Join the Army," and he's thinking to himself, *America's under attack, I gotta sign up*, and then he walks to the voter registration booth next to the recruiter and signs up there.

Delaney Tarr

OUR FIRST TRIP TO DC: FEBRUARY 25

TWO WEEKS AFTER THE SHOOTING, Matt and Ryan Deitsch organized a group of classmates and traveled to Washington, DC. On February 26 and 27, the students met with elected officials to discuss gun reform and visited local kids who were inspired to organize by March for Our Lives.

There was a feeling of hope in the air. It was only two weeks after the shooting when Matt and Ryan selected a group to go to Washington, DC, for the first time. It was a quick trip, only two days, but it was packed full of meetings with elected officials.

Things had been so hectic since we'd first started doing interviews with the media, but somehow, it felt like all of our talk had been building up to these meetings. To have an open conversation with the people who can make real legislative change. We felt like more than just teens.

It was the first time I'd ever stepped foot into Washington, DC. As we drove to our hotel, I was immediately enraptured by the history and life that the city held. This was democracy in action. You could see the Capitol from our hotel, and we all fell in love with the city and all it stood for. We also fell in love with the idea of making change. And I'm not going to fault us for that because it was our first time ever really being in a place that powerful. At least, it was our first time being there with a voice. Everybody always brings up the Tallahassee trip, which was fine and good. We talked to our state legislators and a lot was accomplished. But this was the next level. It gave us a chance to bond. We were all in hotel rooms, hanging out until three in the morning, because we're teenagers and that's how we relax.

There was an undeniable bond and chemistry between us that we didn't get to experience before that. It was only eleven days after the shooting, and activism was still very new to us. Most of us had known each other, but we hadn't bonded as friends. We were just coworkers at the time. I know that I bonded with a very few specific people, and those bonds are still intact today. They've shifted a lot as things have changed and as we've been separated for long periods of time, but ultimately that was the basis for our little family. I think that was the first time that I genuinely felt happy after the shooting.

The first day we went to lobby felt magical in a way. We all crammed into two cars, and were dropped off right near the National Mall. It was a brisk day, not cold, but windy enough that the air felt crisp. Dressed in our best business attire, we stepped up to the Capitol Building, and looked out over the National Mall. The grass was so expansive, so empty, that all we could do was think about what it would look like during the March for Our Lives. To commemorate the moment, we took a picture with us all looking off into the distance. And I think we all felt really powerful there, because it felt like we were there to make real change. That we were getting in there, getting boots on the ground. That we were going to get this legislation written. It was optimistic, it was hopeful.

In that moment, we felt like we could take on the world. We might have been a bit too confident then. Logically, we knew that things wouldn't be so simple, that we couldn't just storm into Congress and get what we wanted. But it was hard to shake that feeling of possibility. We were, after all, scheduled to meet with some of the biggest political figures in Washington.

Of course, that wasn't necessarily what happened when we arrived. As soon as we got to the Capitol Building, we were faced with a labyrinth that left us all disoriented. They had fancy "people movers" to take us from one side of the building to the other. The hallways were winding, with few windows and many doors. We were, to say the least, overwhelmed.

The first person we approached was a California politician who asked us, "What are you doing here?" So we explained to him that we were there with the March for Our Lives, that we were there to lobby for gun reform. At hearing that, his attitude shifted. He immediately started to treat us like kids and was rude to us. We left that impromptu meeting feeling a bit hopeless and disenfranchised, but at the same time fueled to continue.

As we began our meetings, we grew to realize that it's a learning process. We had some of the points that we wanted to talk about, but career politicians aren't exactly the easiest people to communicate with. Unsurprisingly, they would try to manipulate the conversation so they would get to say their piece, and often left us with barely any time to get a word in. Sort of like, "I want to hear what you have to say, but first things first: Here's everything that I think."

At other times, we were listened to, and it was very powerful. We were talking to Senators Lindsey Graham, Paul Ryan, Nancy Pelosi, Chuck Schumer, Bill Nelson, Bernie Sanders, and these huge figures that we've known about and learned about, but never had the chance to actually communicate with. Did they listen to us? Maybe. I can't guarantee they all did, because nothing has really happened yet. One of the best examples of lack of action would probably be with Paul Ryan. We all tried to talk gun control with him, and he just skirted around the topic, favoring a focus on mental health. It was a valid topic, but the moment that Alex Wind brought up a question, namely, "What about the Las Vegas shooter, who had no history of mental health issues?" Ryan responded with a simple "I don't know."

Many of the meetings were demoralizing, but right afterward, we experienced a total shift. We were totally energized from the caffeine we had readily consumed, and went directly into a meeting with Representative John Lewis, who is as close to perfect as a human could get (yes, that was hyperbolic). I think most of us cried, or almost cried, when he was telling us his story. To hear a civil rights activist say, "We support you guys. We stand with you. We marched, now you do your marching. We see so many parallels."

There were reminders of the shooting all around us, though. I remember one legislator went into excruciating detail about the whereabouts of the shooter during the entire shooting. That really brought us back to the moment a lot, and made us realize we weren't fully over it yet. I know that during Nancy Pelosi's meeting, a lot of us didn't know that when they make votes on the floor, there is a loud beeping noise that sounds a lot like a fire alarm. For a lot of us, that kind of triggered us and sent us back to the moment. I remember looking at someone with true fear in my eyes, really panicking, wondering, *Are we going to die?*

Because that was one of those moments when we were confronted with something that truly brought us back there. These people in Washington hadn't been affected by it, so they didn't know that they needed to be more sensitive about it. And that was something that dulled the happiness to see all of us panicking at the same time because we heard a fire drill. We had been living in almost an escape from our reality, but those moments tethered us to what brought us there in the first place.

We were new to all of this. It was a lot of us trying to balance still recovering from our grief, still not being even remotely close to okay, but wanting to be okay. Wanting to be these powerhouses, these superheroes who come in and just save the day. I think a lot of us had that mentality, that we would go in and we would show them. We would show them exactly how common sense everything we are asking for is, and everyone would understand, and we would get at least one thing done. Once again, not necessarily realistic, but I think it was an important thing to have, because we wouldn't have kept going, and we wouldn't be so determined if we didn't have the hope and the optimism. It's mixed in with a lot of pain every day. But it's a necessary feeling to have.

After we met with the legislators, we ended up going to a high school, Blair High School. It was the first high school that we visited. It was the first time that we saw an actual outpouring of support from teenagers that wasn't on social media or the news. This was actual face-to-face, bona fide outreach. We walked into the auditorium not sure what to expect and were immediately given a standing ovation by a completely full auditorium with hundreds of kids. I know that a lot of us cried, because to see all of these teenagers care enough to come out, to give their time and their patience and their ears to listen to us, and to ask us questions, and to just genuinely support us, was so powerful.

The students at Blair High School knew exactly who we were. They wanted to take pictures with us, they wanted to talk to us. They wanted to be our friends. To help. They had organized their own events. They were organizing walkouts and sit-ins because they were close to the Capitol. It was amazing to see the initiative that people were taking without us telling them to take action.

Because we hadn't been able to. We hadn't had the march yet, we hadn't established an outreach infrastructure.

But this was still people taking action, and really being leaders. It's a quote that Matt Deitsch has said many a time: "Leaders create leaders." And that was something that we saw there, in that high school auditorium. We saw leaders in that room full of teenagers, maybe even more so than in the Capitol. In the Capitol we saw people who would dismiss us. People who would say that they agreed with us, or promised us things and then break those promises.

We saw people who were almost untouchable in the way that we spoke to them. We knew that no matter what we said to them, this is their job. They are professional politicians—they've been doing this for years. Their incumbency will likely not be threatened. And that was what the feeling was. It was a mixture of optimism and pessimism that left us feeling pretty middle-of-the-road at the end of the trip.

But things have changed. Things really have changed now. We actually have threatened people's incumbency with voting. Because we realized that no matter how much we want to talk about legislation that we can try and get written and that we can try and get passed, the best way to really make that difference is to get people to vote for the right leaders.

It was cool to meet Bernie Sanders, it was cool to meet John Lewis, but it means a lot more to meet a teenager who says, "You inspired me to create my own march." And that was the big takeaway. We can lobby, we can push for policy, and we have been. We have people in DC on the ground doing that. But the core of this movement is and always will be with young people, instead of with people who are older, and who are getting paid hundreds of thousands of dollars to do this job as public servants. I think that's what's really important to us.

STRONG

BE POSITIVE • BE PASSIONATE • BE PROUD TO BE AN EAGLE

er in our hearts

CARA LOUGHRAN

CARMEN SCHENTRUP

CHRIS HIXON

GINA MONTALTO

MEADOW POLLACK

NICHOLAS DWORET

PETER WANG

SCOTT BEIGEL

4, 2018

THE FIRST DAY BACK AT SCHOOL: FEBRUARY 28

ADAM ALHANTI: There's no handbook for rebuilding after a school shooting. No one knew what to do.

DAVID HOGG: It's like, the best way I can describe it is imagine getting in a plane crash and then having to get on that same plane every day without fixing the problem that caused the plane crash in the first place, and just having to expect, like, "Yeah, it's not going to happen." And learn. You can't. I couldn't.

JOHN BARNITT: Going back on the first day was when I realized that this isn't a thing that's going to go away. This will be with us forever. Those six minutes on February 14 will be with us forever. It's weird to think that we even had to have a first day back after a shooting. We went to this place for years, and then you have to be reintroduced to this school you've called a home.

JACLYN CORIN: We only got two weeks off, which was surprising to me. A lot of kids weren't ready. Personally, I was ready to go back just because I wanted to be in that environment. I wanted to be surrounded by other people because I didn't want to be alone. But it wasn't really fair for some people.

KYRAH SIMON: I had a lot of anxiety. I was debating if I wanted to go or if I wanted to stay home. There were a lot of people who thought it was better to stay home rather than go back that soon.

RYAN DEITSCH: There was a funeral on the first orientation day back. That same day. And they had teachers coming in anyway. Whether you were going to every funeral or not, they were still happening all around you. It still hadn't ended. Yet they were acting like it had.

ADAM: The first thing you were supposed to do that first day back was to get your stuff, because we'd all left without our backpacks and the rest of our things that day. So first I went to the last class I was in, to get my bag and my laptop, and whatever else I had left behind that day. I remember there was still Valentine's

Day stuff in the room I went into. Teddy bears, valentines, saggy half-deflated helium balloons—at the point where they're not floating, but not on the floor.

ALFONSO CALDERON: Usually I drive to school, but my mom wanted to drive me back. You know how parents are.

DANIEL WILLIAMS: My mom and I share a car. I wanted to drive my siblings to school on our first day back, but my mom really insisted on driving us. My brother Andrew is a sophomore and my sister Vanessa is a freshman. Normally I'd push back, but I understood. She needed to see her kids off to school on our first day back.

ADAM: Usually in the morning, when school starts, there's this roar of kids eating breakfast and talking with their friends, and the rush of finishing homework. But on that day it was silent. Not a single person was speaking.

JOHN: I walked those halls every day—that's where my teachers were, that's where I was growing relationships, going to clubs—school was a happy place. It was still the same school, same hallways, but the energy transformed. The place I used to think of as my happy little school had completely transformed into a place where crying echoed through the hallways. No one knew how to act because no one had ever been through it before—we were all going through it at the same time.

DANIEL: That first day wasn't about getting back into a routine, it was just about being comfortable being in the building again. My walk into school that day followed the same evacuation route I had to take on February 14. I had to retrace those steps. It was an eerie feeling to be in some of those same spots, but this time things looked a lot different. There were flowers everywhere and signs people had made. We were surrounded by support.

ALFONSO: It was like a circus. I expected a big to-do for the kids, but it was almost ridiculous. It felt like there were six hundred police officers, which was good because we needed the police officers, but also kind of ridiculous. I got dropped off, I walked across the street, and all of the police officers were just cheering and smiling, saying, "Welcome back!" It was nice and comforting, but at the same time it felt kind of disrespectful, in my opinion. Seventeen people died there two weeks before that day. Two weeks. It felt like everybody was pretending like nothing happened.

SARAH CHADWICK: I just remember just walking in and there were poodles and dogs everywhere and just like, seeing the school, there was like police officers lined up with flowers, and the police officers were giving us flowers, all in a line as we passed by.

CHRIS GRADY: We knew that it was important we go back, so we did, and I knew I kind of had to go back to be there for a lot of my friends who were scared about going back. The whole street leading up to the school was just filled with cop cars, and I don't know, I think they were trying to do a show of strength, but it just kind of—it rubbed me the wrong way.

DELANEY TARR: It wasn't a day of education by any means. But it was probably one of the more therapeutic experiences that I've had. I can't say that that's true for everyone, but for me school was one of the few places that I didn't feel I had to put on this face for the media. Where I didn't feel like I had to explain myself constantly because even with your family, they are affected by it, but they aren't in it. So they don't necessarily know. At school I was around, especially in my newspaper class, people who were there. The people who I was with during the shooting. And that definitely made me feel more comfortable, and more able to be vulnerable without criticizing it or saying that I'm doing it for the cameras, without having to put on that brave face and switch into interview mode, or speech mode, or legislator mode, or anything like that. It was just, I could be myself. Genuinely, truly, who I was before the shooting, who I am after the shooting. I didn't have to try and be anything.

DANIEL: I was glad to be with my friends because you could have an open conversation with them. People assume you don't want to talk about it, but it helps to talk about it. Everyone shared where they were. Some people were far away, some people happened to leave thirty seconds before the shooting started.

RYAN: The only solace I found was seeing my friends. The only good thing about it was the therapy dogs. The dogs were cute.

DANIEL: In our first period we played with Play-Doh. In our second period we painted rocks. There were therapy dogs everywhere. It really helped. I heard the principal say, "You think this is a lot of dogs? Wait until tomorrow." There were dogs there all week.

DAVID: I didn't know how to feel about it, I just did it. And for me it was just sad the first couple days because we were like toddlers. We were playing with Play-Doh and coloring and shit and, like, that was tough to see. There was a lot of posters around that helped a lot. Therapy dogs were probably the most helpful thing for our school.

KEVIN TREJOS: A strategy I've used throughout this experience is that I've dealt with it by sort of hiding behind my camera. I was already back at the school by February 15 or 16, taking photos that I knew would be used in the paper. The excuse of going to take photos for journalism reasons helped me deal with what had happened there. So that day, like before, I brought my camera. I was probably the only person in the school with a DSLR since they didn't let media in. That helped me deal with stuff.

ADAM: At that point we didn't know if we were taking AP exams, and our finals were in a few weeks. We all wanted to know, but the teachers kept saying not to worry about it.

JACLYN: We had no idea if we had to take AP exams, we just had no idea what we were walking into. We didn't know what was going to happen to our grades. I took a test on Valentine's Day and I didn't know if it was going to count.

RYAN: I'm in TV production class and one of the assignments before the shooting was making a short PSA. I filmed the PSA on February 13, and I had not touched my camera since that day. Our teacher set a due date when we returned, but when I started to look at all of this footage of us before the tragedy, it was just too hard. The teacher understood and that project was canceled. I share that class with David Williams and Delaney Tarr, and we were working on those projects together. Looking at footage of us before the shooting, before any of this, it was really difficult.

JACLYN: There were just so many things going through my head, me being an academic nerd, that I was just worrying about school and then I thought, "Why am I worrying about school?"

I was stressed because I had so much March for Our Lives stuff to do and I thought, "I can't be here. I need to be in the office."

RYAN: Since I had joined this group and we had been doing a lot of important activism work, sitting down in a classroom almost felt wasteful. I mean just in the first couple of weeks being back, there was the shooting in Yountville, California, at the Pathway Home, a non-profit PTSD program at the Veterans Home of California. I was speaking to people from Yountville while I was in math class. It was a difficult balance to strike. I didn't want to let anyone down, but I still needed to live my life as a high school student.

EMMA GONZÁLEZ: I don't actually remember first day back where all the classes were because it was really difficult, nothing made sense, 'cause like nobody in the freshman building was able to go back to their classes, obviously.

KEVIN: We walked in through the side of the school across from the freshman building. We could see that they'd boarded up windows that were shot through. They'd also blocked everything off.

CHRIS: They had panels over the windows that had bullet holes in them.

ADAM: I parked in the senior lot, which is right next to the freshman building, where the shooting took place. I got out of my car and we had to go to one of the three entrances—they had us use the one next to the freshman building. There were probably about a thousand of us going in at that point, and we all had to walk past that building. That was probably the harshest moment for me. It's the closest I'd been to the building since that day.

DANIEL: They built a huge fence around the freshman building. I walked past the building several times each day, so seeing it now with windows boarded up was pretty shocking. The first class I ever had at MSD was in that building. I thought back to that classroom, I have a vivid memory of that class, my first high school class. I had fond memories there. It's the staple of our school; it's the first building you see. Now they are going to knock it down.

ADAM: A few days later we had to go get our cars back from the lot, and I remember walking as far from the freshman building as I could. If the parking lot was twenty feet wide, and the building was to the left, I was on the right. There was no chance I was getting close to it. I tried my hardest to avoid it during that period of time, although of course when we went back for real, there wasn't really any way to avoid it.

KYRAH: They fenced off the freshman 1200 building—obviously, we can never go back there. There are so many teachers without classrooms. I had my psychology class in the same class as my history class. You could see anger and pain in teachers' faces. Everything had changed for them too.

DANIEL: We started the day off with fourth period, which was when the shooting happened. I really appreciated that they did that, it helped get it over with.

DELANEY: I know that a lot of us in my newspaper class, because that's where I was during the shooting, made a point of trying to go in the closet that first day because that's where we were hiding during it. To just try and not relive it but see, can we even function as normal people anymore, have we healed at all, can we continue to heal? And that's what the day was.

CAMERON KASKY: Trauma is one thing we all share.

DAVID: The main thing I did, was I just went out to Marjory's Garden, where I was working the morning of the shooting. I'd created this hydroponics thing with some of the teachers, and I'd planted a bunch of peas that morning in there and now they had grown into full-blown plants with, like, peas everywhere. So I went out there and harvested those, and just sat out there in the sun and just listened, you know? It's a very calming and therapeutic area of our school.

RYAN: The first week back, they had police officers holding the same weapon our shooter used. I don't know who made that decision, but they were on the corner of every building. It made the school feel like a prison colony. The most ridiculous part, which I saw from the highway and from my astronomy class, was the garden. The astronomy classroom overlooks the garden. The astronomy teacher had worked on that garden for several years, and students helped. David loved it there. There were two officers holding semiautomatic weapons protecting the garden. The garden! No threat, no evil, just flowers and AR-15s.

KYRAH: Those first few days back were a mix of comfort and anxiety. I knew that things would never be normal again, school would never feel normal again, so I would have to get adjusted to a new normal. To me, the increased security—police officers everywhere, walking around with AR-15s—that was a real symbol of the fact that things will never be the same. They added fencing and barricades everywhere, they gave us clear backpacks. They transformed the way our school functioned and then claimed that we were getting back to normal. Get back to academics, study for your SATs. And walking around campus, it just wasn't normal.

JOHN: A lot of people wanted to go back to normal. They just wanted structure in their life and they wanted school to just go back to being school, but there were other people who needed that time to heal. But since our school is so big, you can't decide, and you don't know when it's a healthy time to slowly start going back to some normality. I feel like the school did the best that they could, slowly bringing us back into some structure and to a regular day of school.

CAMERON: The best feeling in the entire world was seeing my teachers. This whole tragedy had a life-altering impact for everyone involved, but the teaching staff still had to do their jobs. They were just as brave as we were for coming back to school. We had two weeks off, but they had one. They went right back and they got ready. They were selfless. They only cared about us. I never understood the degree to which teachers care for their students until the shooting. They were there for us and it was so moving to me.

SOFIE WHITNEY: I think a lot of people don't realize that while obviously the kids were all completely shaken up by everything that happened, even if they weren't in the building, the teachers had the same experience as us. They're humans. They don't have a special part of their brains that made them better suited to be in that situation than we were. I think people don't realize how much it affected them.

ALFONSO: On the first day back, Mr. Levine, my English teacher, kicked off the discussion by asking, "Can humankind achieve peace?" to kids who just went through something antithetical to peace, kids who were unsure. He basically wanted to inspire us to think about that question and write something about how we were feeling. His message was that peace can be achieved even if people don't know what to do.

There were a lot of kids in that class who were saying, "We've gotta make schools like prisons. We have to get fences and metal detectors. We need soldiers." More of this, more of that. I remember thinking, everyone is entitled to their opinion, but how is that supposed to fix everything? I didn't really argue either, I wasn't in the mood to say anything. I'd spoken out for two weeks. I just hung my head low, but at the end of class, I thanked Mr. Levine for talking about something that is sensitive but much needed. I had wished that in any other class, a teacher had the balls to say, "Hey, kids, this happened. Now we have to think about it and move through it."

SARAH: In sociology class, every morning when we do attendance the teacher asks a question and we answer it individually, and that's how he takes attendance. I remember that his question that day was "Do you feel safe?" and a lot of people honestly answered, "No, I don't feel safe." Because, no, of course we don't feel safe. I mean, we have therapy dogs, we have armed security everywhere, but the fact that it happened is still lingering in the back of our minds, and it will always be there.

JOHN: I was used to my teachers talking about what you're doing that day, if you have a test, what you're studying that week. And that day was completely different. They were saying things like, "We're going to get through this. We're going to do anything we can to make this an easier transition." And to see all my teachers who I looked up to, now turned to these real people. Because they're affected by it too. They have emotions, they might not know how to feel, and they were upset and crying too.

CAMERON: Ernest Rospierski was a teacher in the freshman building. The shooter came right by his door. Mr. Rospierski is one of my favorite teachers. His classroom was right next to Scott Beigel's classroom, and I know they were friends. He was extremely dedicated to his students and to teaching before the shooting, but even more so afterward. I didn't think that was possible.

DANIEL: All the teachers were very supportive. They didn't know what to do either. The shooting impacted them as much as it had us. No one wanted to jump back into the curriculum. We couldn't just gloss over it and get back to work. I remember hugging a lot of teachers, even teachers from past years. Even if you didn't like the teacher, everyone was just happy to see each other. The teachers just wanted us to know that all they cared about was our mental and physical health. They were so understanding.

JOHN: A moment I really remember is seeing my teacher Mr. Schaller. He always has a smile on his face, he laughs, he tells jokes, and he's a great teacher, but he's also very professional. He has such a structure to his class. He was one of my favorite teachers that year, and just walking up to him and saying hello like I always would and seeing how vulnerable he was that day, you saw that he cared about his students and that he felt like he failed his students. He didn't know what to do. He gave me a hug, which was so weird to me because usually I would walk into class, sit down, and say hi and that's it. Seeing him be more of a friend than my teacher . . . It's breaking that barrier between student and teacher and being this group of people who endured something so tragic and having school be reshaped as not just a place of learning but also a place of coping.

RYAN: Some teachers were angry, some didn't want to come back, others were acting like nothing had happened at all. And you can't pretend that nothing has happened when you look down the school hallways and every high school, middle school, and elementary school in the country has sent a banner that says, "We're standing with you." The writing is literally on the walls that shows that this isn't normal, that this shouldn't have happened. To come back after two weeks, it's like nothing.

ALEX WIND: My calculus teacher said probably the most insightful thing I heard at the time. He said that right now, everything is like a snow globe. When you shake up a snow globe, all the little flakes fly around and everything is chaos, but eventually, the flakes settle. That first day back, we were settling into that new normal.

JACLYN: When I got back to the classroom I was hiding in, it was a weird experience, because I had been filled with so much fear and the last time I saw the room, there was glass all over the floor and members of the SWAT team with guns that were bigger than me. Now, it was as if nothing had happened. The rooms were back to the way they were, and the walls were plastered with posters from schools and communities around the world sending us well wishes.

DANIEL: My experience was sort of unique because on the day of the shooting, I wasn't in my fourth-period class, I was in the auditorium. I have drama class fourth period, so I was in the auditorium working on the sound design for the musical. When we decided as a class that we were still going to do the play, it meant that I had to go right back to doing what I was doing when the shooting happened, but being in the auditorium again allowed me to collect my thoughts. I sat onstage by myself. The curtain was down, and I could hear people sitting in the auditorium. I let it all in.

KYRAH: That first day back, Helena Ramsay's absence was really hard on me. We were friends since kindergarten. We have a block schedule, so four double periods a day. We call them silver days and burgundy days for our school colors. The silver days were like something I had to get through, like green peas on your plate. The burgundy day was the mashed potatoes and macaroni. That was my day. I had two periods with Helena. I had all my favorite classes that day. I hated trigonometry, but I had trigonometry with Helena, she sat right behind me. Me, Helena, and my friend Carson would literally talk the entire class. The teacher would always crack on us, but she loved us. I also had AP US History with Helena, and we never really sat near each other, but when there was a group project we would sync up like magnets. I loved bothering Helena. It was my favorite thing to do.

They switched up the desks in trigonometry, but from that first day back to the last day of school, when I would look behind me, nobody would be there. I could just feel her absence. Even after moving around desks, she was still the only one missing. Everyone else in the class was still there, still coming to school, but Helena was never coming back.

JOHN: The first class I went to was my drama class. I liked going to that class first, because that was my home base before all of this. That was a lot of our home bases in this movement. It was nice going back there, seeing familiar faces, seeing my teachers, and actually settling in before going to all my other classes.

ADAM: For me, the first class was AP Psychology. The teacher sat there and looked at us and said, "I am so sorry," and cried. We had taken a test that day, and she told us not to worry about it. We had a project coming up, and she said not to worry about it. She passed around notecards and asked us to write what we wanted to get out of the class. So we passed in the notecards anonymously. Some kids said they didn't want to come to school, to do work, to bring their backpacks. Other kids said they wanted things to go back to normal.

EMMA: After fourth period, we went to first period, which for me was personalization [a study hall]. For the rest of the year, they combined all personalization classes and held them in the auditorium, which was where I was during the shooting. I was forced to go there every other day.

SARAH: My second period was originally in the freshman building where it happened, but that day we went to a different classroom; my teacher just talked about what she went through during it, because she was in the building. Something that I noticed is that a lot of my teachers rearranged the desks into a circle, because they thought it was going to be a "talk about your feelings" time, and my teacher stood in the middle of the circle and asked if anyone had anything to say and encouraged us to talk about how we were feeling. It was very emotional, obviously, every single period.

KEVIN: Third period was a tough class for me. Three kids in that class weren't there. One, Carmen Schentrup, had died, one was recovering from gunshots, and another was out because his brother died. The class was AP English Lit, one of the hardest in school, and all the kids in that class have known each other for a really long time. We all had known Carmen for years, and we were all pretty good friends. So there were a lot of empty desks, and that made it hard.

The teacher made us do an activity to get us to talk. She gave us a ball of string; we had to say how we were feeling when it was tossed to us. I wasn't a fan of that, because I don't like when teachers or other people try to force feelings out of us, especially in that class. That class was really awkward because of the empty desks.

We wanted to do something to honor Carmen. We put flowers on her desk, and someone made a poster. But still, it's just a desk. It's not the only one she ever sat in, and it's not like she was only in that seat for that entire year. So I don't know that it made me feel any better.

The next day we came back and rearranged the entire classroom. We tried to forget where her desk would have been, to get the thought out of our minds, because otherwise looking at that desk would bring up memories of who should be there. I used to sit right behind her. The first thing I did was decide I wasn't sitting in that seat anymore. I didn't want to deal with that. So I moved seats.

SOFIE: I remember getting to fifth period, and knowing that the teacher in that class was the only teacher I had that had a victim currently in their class. Carmen Schentrup was his student. He broke down in front of the whole class. That was really sad. You go to school and see your teachers every day, but you never think about what it's like to sit in your classroom as your teacher's crying. It's not a normal thing. That happened a few times that day.

ALFONSO: In sixth period, my math class, I was faced with my very conservative teacher. He had a discussion with a student who was unprepared, somebody who agreed with our viewpoints, but didn't know enough to back them up. I didn't want to be angry that day, but that did piss me off.

ALEX: I went into my statistics class seventh period, which Carmen Schentrup was a student in. It was such a strange, sad feeling, walking into that classroom and seeing that she wasn't there. We were all just sharing stories and talking about what had happened. It turned into a celebration and a remembrance of her. It wasn't about the tragedy, it was about how do we lift everything up, how do we make sure that we can remember Carmen and the other victims.

JACLYN: Some of my teachers weren't as gentle as others. Once we started getting back into academics and doing the walkouts, some teachers disagreed with us, or at least what I stood for, which was kind of disheartening. Seeing a teacher who went through that experience with us saying, "What's the point of a walkout?" And I was like, "Do you know the history of protests in this country?"

CAMERON: In one of my last classes of the day, I had a panic attack. I had become a notable figure in the movement, and the first day back was hard for me. It was overwhelming and I felt so anxious. It got into my head that someone had poisoned me. I felt like I couldn't breathe, I was gasping for air, I was seeing spots. I thought I was going to die. I wound up in the hospital, where they explained to me what was happening. After I calmed down, I immediately thought about getting back to work. I had a movement to run. It's hard to sit in class and do work that's unrelated to the movement.

EMMA: Each class period was kind of different. Like maybe one was all breakdowns and maybe one was all . . . not fun, but a little easier. A lot of us were saying to ourselves, "I don't want to cry right now," and then others thought, "I can't stop crying right now." It comes in waves.

JACLYN: It'll be hard for the sophomore class next year because they have three years left, but I'm going to be a senior and so I only have one more year left. I'm going to be class president again as well so I'm going to try my best to make all the new-comers feel very welcome because it must be hard to walk into a school that had a shooting last year, so I'm going to try my best to make everyone feel good about going to school here. But it's going to be hard. Once the freshman class from this year graduates, I think it's going to be a little easier for people, but for the next couple years, we're going to have to be very gentle, and nonpolitical and just focus on ourselves and grieving and our counselors. We're always going to have therapy dogs, which is nice. I love that.

arlie Mirsky
Douglas High School,
rkland, Florida

Charlie Mirsky

DIRECT POLITICAL PRESSURE: EARLY MARCH

CHARLIE MIRSKY, A FORMER STUDENT of teacher Scott Beigel, discusses joining March for Our Lives as the only non-MSD student and his role in supporting the movement and amplifying the stories of gun violence survivors.

My mission to incite change in our country began in a unique way. Unlike the rest of the founders of the movement, I was never a student at Marjory Stoneman Douglas. I got involved after the shooting through my connection with Scott Beigel and friendship with Cameron Kasky. I've known Cameron since we were in kindergarten—we were best friends when we went to elementary school together. It's funny because I remember clearly that we were the only first graders who cared about politics. Cameron was complaining about the system when we were practically toddlers. We weren't really informed when we were six years old, but we followed elections and had opinions even then.

Cameron and I were in the same fifth-grade class at that school, and our teacher was Scott Beigel, who died at Marjory

Stoneman Douglas protecting his high school students. I remember Mr. Beigel being a really cool teacher in elementary school. Even when we were just ten and eleven years old, he pushed us to understand the world outside of our little bubble. He referenced a lot of things that I didn't know about. We would chat about politics a lot, which was cool for a fifth-grade teacher to do.

I only had Scott Beigel for fifth grade, and didn't talk to him much after that. But his character stayed with me. Even now, I can guarantee that every one of his students got to experience his wit, sarcasm, and charisma. Cameron left that school after fifth grade, but he and I stayed friends. I would get in touch with him after months and the friendship wouldn't feel different.

After I heard about the shooting, I sent Cameron a message asking if he was safe. Not long after that, he called me. The group he created wanted to do something in response to the shooting, and I asked if they had ideas. They said, "We think we should organize a march on DC. There are a lot of cameras on us, so we can make this a big deal." He asked me to help because I'm organized, but also because I'm so politically minded.

At first, I wasn't sure whether I would have a place in a movement like that. I knew Cameron and had known Mr. Beigel, but I wasn't personally a survivor of the shooting. But I agreed to get involved, and ever since that night, I became a dedicated member of March for Our Lives. While I was aware of my status as an outsider when I joined the Douglas kids, they welcomed me in immediately. I've stayed aware that they've been through something really traumatic that I haven't, and I try to keep that in mind, especially when I've done media appearances. Sometimes news outlets would mistakenly identify me as a survivor of the shooting, which is frustrating even though I know it's probably because I've been helping out since the beginning.

I started out by helping to organize events such as the CNN Town Hall, doing my own media appearances, and helping other kids with speeches and talking points for their interviews. I wrote questions for Cameron and Emma ahead of the CNN Town Hall. That was a cool moment because I got to see the things I've written get shared with the world. That was when things started to feel really big and real. You know when kids get together with their friends and make a grand plan—like to make a movie, or start a business? At first, the movement felt a little like that, because we're so young and didn't really know what we were doing. But we figured out how to get our message out and grow our support. That started to happen in the weeks after the shooting, and those few weeks were the craziest of my life.

As the movement has grown, my involvement has shifted a bit. I've been using my organizational skills and deep political knowledge to help change gun reform policy. I remember that when the shooting happened, everyone was upset. I was too, and I was especially sad about Mr. Beigel. But I was also frustrated with some people, especially the people who were empowered to prevent the shooting if they had been motivated to do it. I thought, *come on*. I knew exactly who was responsible the moment it happened, and I considered it murder on the part of the people who let it happen—especially Florida and federal politicians. They know the risks that come with our gun laws—there are statistics that they have fought in Congress to keep from the public. You don't hide a statistic unless you know it's bad. So I was really upset and motivated to hold them accountable. That's a big part of why I was so excited to join the movement.

Cameron and I were always interested in politics, and I credit my dad for encouraging my interest from a young age. My dad studied political science at Johns Hopkins and then at Princeton, and on some issues I'd say he's better informed than anyone I know to this day, even more than politicians. That's pretty shocking. I thought legislators like Bernie Sanders would know more than my dad about gun policy, but I've learned that's not the case.

In any case, my dad always taught me about politics, but I started paying attention more around my sophomore year of high school, a year and a half ago. My friend Nathaniel introduced me to the *New York Times* and TV hosts like John Oliver and Stephen Colbert, people whom I watched for fun but also helped me get informed. They were a reliable source of information about what was going on in the country politically, but at the end of the day they're still comedians. The *New York Times* is The News, more formally. Nathaniel also helped me read college studies, and I started reading books about politics. A major point of interest for me is corruption in government—which ties into our cause in a big way—and so are problems with high partisanship levels. When it comes to specific issues, I've been interested in the environment and conservation, and I was passionate about gun reform even before the shooting in Parkland.

Since those first few weeks, and the march, my job has vastly expanded. I feel like it's more important to hear these stories from the kids who were at Marjory Stoneman Douglas. But as someone who wasn't a student there, I've found my way to contribute is through direct political pressure and talking to lawmakers directly about policy. It was great at the start when I was helping with the media strategy and talking points, but I also felt like we have major trouble in the House and the Senate. That's become a focus for me, since we've had so many opportunities to meet with politicians. That kind of thing bores a lot of kids, but I like it. When we'd do interviews or meet politicians on the ground, I would get their chief of staff's contact info and work to set up meetings to talk about policy.

By the date of the march, I'd built a pretty big network of names in Tallahassee and in DC. Probably one that's worth something. I want to leverage these connections because not everybody has them, and it's an important way to effect change. I've continued to build my network of politicians, and my job now is to connect with them and push legislation that March for Our Lives believes in. I don't like to call myself a lobbyist, but that's sort of what I've become. I represent the organization in any way I can. While the entire movement is having an effect on the public conversation around gun reform, I'm the group's link to the politicians themselves.

I've found that I'm pretty good at that work too. Just a few months after the shooting, I feel like I have a pretty strong footing in Congress, and I'm still only in high school. My work can help us score legislative victories and harness the energy of the group to change the way Congress deals with guns. I see myself as the more low-key persuasive counterpart to the more public-facing, energetic style that people like David Hogg have. We need both kinds of activism to push the changes we want: the passionate energy and the more focused, one-on-one argument.

And I really have done that: met one-on-one with major figures in the Senate and House to push legislation, like digitizing the gun records held by the Bureau of Alcohol, Tobacco, Firearms and Explosives, which has been my main issue recently. I'm proud that I helped write and put together the press release for the ATF digitization bill called the Crime Gun Tracing Modernization Act that Senators Bill Nelson and Patrick Leahy released in May 2018.

I'm especially passionate about this bill and issue because it's so hard to square opposition to it with the "law and order" stance we see so often in politics. It seems like a no-brainer to me: digitizing existing records doesn't put gun owners at risk unless their guns are used to commit violent crimes, and it would help law enforcement to respond more effectively to gun violence. It's crazy to me that we have these records, but they're only allowed right now to be kept on paper. From a conservative standpoint, all I can think is, *Don't you guys like to support police officers?* It's a perfect example of the kind of commonsense reform that would save lives and would have bipartisan support if it wasn't for conspiratorial opposition from groups like the NRA.

Working on issues like this has become my role in the organization, so in the summer of 2018, while most of the March for Our Lives founders headed out for a statewide tour of Florida and a nationwide tour across the entire United States, I've decided to stay in DC where I can be most effective personally. Especially now, with midterm elections and Supreme Court issues coming up in 2018, working with Congress on both sides of the aisle feels vitally important.

And I do mean it when I say I want to work with politicians on both sides of the spectrum. It's not just Democrats. Republicans in office, and new candidates, can prove themselves to us by backing gun reform and representing the people the way we want them to. It's that simple. I don't care what your title is. If you support what we support, that's good.

Unfortunately, with Republicans in control of the House and Senate, so far they've stayed firmly on the side of the gun lobby, and I don't think we can get anything meaningful done until that changes, whether it's through a Democratic wave or by electing Republicans more open to commonsense reform than the ones we have now. For now, I'm all about building relationships with candidates and currently serving politicians. I've gotten to know the leadership of both parties, and I've met with Republicans like Jeff Flake, Lisa Murkowski, Paul Ryan, and Peter King, but I know that nothing is going to happen unless things change. I can't singlehandedly change their minds, but I can take these opportunities to hold them accountable. For example, if Marco Rubio refuses to support commonsense reforms, I can use that stance on record, along with my own platform, to support his opposition. And it's not hard to get these people to say things that we can use against them in the name of lifesaving reforms.

I'm also ready to put the pressure on senators when it comes to the Supreme Court. With Justice Anthony Kennedy retiring in July 2018, I'm going to do everything I can to persuade senators like Jeff Flake, whom I know well, not to just go with whomever President Trump chooses first. Even if we don't like to admit it as a nation, the Supreme Court really is partisan, and if the GOP has control over it, we have less ability to enact and enforce meaningful gun reform.

That's not to say that we're a partisan group—like I said, we'll support anyone who agrees with our platform, regardless of party. There are Republicans in the March for Our Lives leadership (although some have switched parties after seeing how our Republican representatives responded to our efforts after the shooting). But at the end of the day, it's about staying informed as voters and putting pressure on our representatives to work for us, not groups like the gun lobby. That's what I've been proud to do, and what I plan to continue working on.

Naomi Wadler

THE WALKOUT: MARCH 14

AFTER THE SHOOTING at Marjory Stoneman Douglas, fifth grader Naomi Wadler wanted to make an impact in her own city of Alexandria, Virginia. So she organized the George Mason Elementary School walkout on Wednesday, March 14, the day that students and teachers from over 2,500 schools across America participated in the national school walkout to demand that lawmakers pass legislation that addresses the epidemic of gun violence.

Right after the Stoneman shooting, I saw all of those students acting on their beliefs and contributing to the movement, and I wanted to join in and make an impact myself and within my community in Alexandria, Virginia. The day after the shooting, I talked with my friend Carter Anderson and suggested that we go to the principal to discuss a walkout at George Mason Elementary School, where we both attend fifth grade. We wanted the principal's support, but we were determined to organize a walkout no matter what.

He turned us down. He said that we needed parental supervision for something like that; that it wasn't appropriate for young people our age to just walk out of school. I politely enlightened him to the fact that students don't have parental supervision when they are being shot in their own classrooms. Even though we got a no, we knew we were going for his support, not his permission.

After that initial rejection, we gathered with our friends whom we knew would support the cause and immediately started planning for the national student walkout on March 14. We had meetings during recess, we started a petition, we made signs. Our numbers were increasing and we were becoming stronger. We discussed the expectations: It wasn't recess time. You weren't participating to get out of school. We planned to be silent during the walkout and not do any chants that would interrupt classes still going on inside. We weren't going to give anyone a hard time for not participating. You don't have to agree with people, but you do have to respect them.

We were in the middle of planning on March 7 when I came home from school and my mom told me about the shooting in Birmingham, Alabama. A seventeen-year-old student, Courtlin Arrington, was shot and killed at school. When black girls and women are shot, their names aren't remembered. Carter and I came up with the idea to add a minute to the walkout, so we could honor Courtlin and show that she does matter.

Students across the country participated in the national walkout, but the fact that we were eleven years old and the fact that we added a minute to honor a black teenager—that got us some attention. The day of the walkout, *The Guardian* interviewed Carter and me, and a media company, Now This, saw the interview and created a video with me and Carter and that went pretty viral. After the video started going around, I got invited to speak at the March for Our Lives.

To say that speaking at the march was nerve-wracking would be an understatement. I was really excited and I was really nervous. But I was so encouraged to have this platform and speak to that many people. It was a big opportunity, and that's part of the reason I couldn't turn it down. Speaking to that many people on national television and in front of an audience of half a million people, being able to share my message and my personal story, all of that was really important to me. I think it's important to inspire other black girls and to reach out to other black girls and to encourage them, and for them to know that they have worth. Because if you start there, then you reduce gun violence in those communities. Since the black community is disproportionately affected by this and black women are so affected by this, I think if you start there, it can be a stepping stone to helping other communities. Parkland is an upper-middle-class community and people thought it couldn't happen there, but gun violence happens everywhere.

THE MARCH FOR OUR LIVES: MARCH 24

JACLYN CORIN: After the Tallahassee trip was finally complete, we immediately began planning the March for Our Lives. The whole month was a whirlwind; we worked day in and day out planning logistics, organizing talent and speakers, facilitating the sibling marches, and talking to volunteers. I had never truly set aside time to heal at this point—my mind was solely focused on getting a job done.

Every day that we were planning the march, I got more and more motivated. People cared about this issue. I distinctly remember the day we hit eight hundred sibling marches, some of which were being held in Mumbai, Japan, Australia, and all over Europe. The support from all over the world felt too good to be true. The epicenter of the world for that month was Parkland, my small hometown of 30,000.

JOHN BARNITT: A small town in Florida were the ones who created this. And to be a part of that—I know I'm a part of this movement, but I feel like I've been viewing all of it from an outside perspective. Like it's not as big as it is. I still feel like a small kid in a small town. But these nobodies, we're the ones who were able to get one of the most historic marches to happen.

BRADLEY THORNTON: I remember the night before being very, very excited. All of us were packed in a room together, being idiots, getting speeches 100 percent. I remember pretty vividly walking into Alex Wind's room at the hotel in DC. I think it was Jackie who was reading her speech out loud, finishing up her speech, and it was wonderful. We were all freaking out and clapping along. We took a second to relax, take everything in. This is it, we're here, we did this.

JOHN: Waking up that morning, it still didn't feel real. It was very surreal that it was finally the day we had all been working toward. The day that we had spent hours upon hours thinking about: the march.

SARAH CHADWICK: I just remember all I had to eat that day was coffee, because I was too nervous to eat.

RYAN DEITSCH: We were at most three degrees removed from everyone on Earth. Everyone from the local paper to the

Vatican was talking about what was happening. I still can't comprehend that scale.

DANIEL WILLIAMS: It meant a lot to see so many high schoolers from around the country come to DC to support us. There were kids everywhere. This was truly a young people's march. I'm sad that it took a tragedy at my school for me to get so involved in this cause, but it means a lot that young people across the country saw what happened, heard us speak out, and wanted to stand alongside us that day.

SOFIE WHITNEY: We had no idea what to expect in that moment, either, because we hadn't really been outside. We didn't see the entire crowd until we got out there after breakfast, and it was so packed you couldn't see down the block. There were about 800,000 people in town for the march, but from where we were at first we could see maybe two thousand. It was a never-ending stream of people.

RYAN: Everyone just seemed human. No one seemed above anybody else. They were all there to support us; they were all there for the same reason. The whole day had that unifying feeling. It was a cold day; I was wearing two shirts, but when I got on stage and I looked out into the crowd, I could see the heat waves, just radiating off of them. So many people, packed tight. They created so much heat that you could see it. For miles. From looking out at that crowd and from being in the crowd, you could just feel it. There was an air of hope and the possibility that one day everything would change.

DAVID HOGG: I will tell you, the one thing I'm always going to remember about the march is looking out over the crowd and seeing the mirage of heat rise off of it. That, and not seeing the edge of it.

AN EXCERPT FROM DAVID HOGG'S SPEECH:

I'm gonna start off by putting this price tag right here as a reminder for you guys to know how much Marco Rubio took for every student's life in Florida. One dollar and five cents.

The cold grasp of corruption shackles the District of Columbia. The winter is over. Change is here. The sun shines on a new day, and the day is ours. First-time voters show up 18 percent of the time at mid-term elections. Not anymore. Now, who here is gonna vote in the 2018 election? If you listen real close, you can hear the people in power shaking. They've gotten used to being protective of their position, the safety of inaction. Inaction is no longer safe. And to that, we say: no more.

Ninety-six people die every day from guns in our country, yet most representatives have no public stance on guns. And to that, we say: no more. We are going to make this the voting issue. We are going to take this to every election, to every state, in every city. We are going to make sure the best people get in our elections to run, not as politicians, but as Americans. Because this—this is not cutting it. When people try to suppress your vote, and there are people who stand against you because you're too young, we say: no more.

When politicians say that your voice doesn't matter because the NRA owns them, we say: no more. When politicians send their thoughts and prayers with no action, we say: no more. And to those politicians supported by the NRA, that allow the continued slaughter of our children and our future, I say: get your résumés ready.

Today is the beginning of spring, and tomorrow is the beginning of democracy. Now is the time to come together, not as Democrats, not as Republicans, but as Americans. Americans of the same flesh and blood, that care about one thing and one thing only, and that's the future of this country and the children that are going to lead it.

They will try to separate us in demographics. They will try to separate us by religion, race, congressional district, and class. They will fail. We will come together. We will get rid of these public servants that only serve the gun lobby, and we will save lives. You are those heroes.

Let's put the USA over the NRA. This is the start of the spring and the blossoming of our democracy. So let's take this to our local legislators, and let's take this to midterm elections, because without the persistence—heat—without the persistence of voters and Americans everywhere, getting out to every election, democracy will not flourish. But it can, and it will. So, I say to those politicians that say change will not come, I say: we will not stop until every man, every woman, every child, and every American can live without fear of gun violence. And to that, I say: no more.

DYLAN BAIERLEIN: That view is something that I will never forget. I will never forget the first time I walked onto that stage and saw that massive crowd. It faded away into the distance, filling the horizon with signs, faces, smiles, and tears. I was breathless.

ALFONSO CALDERON: The people from Sandy Hook told us they wanted to hand over a banner from Newtown to someone from Parkland and asked us who that should be. I took a knee like Tim Tebow and was like, of course, I gotta do this. So, I walked out on stage and they handed me the banner and I held it in front of me for a while. The one thing that shocked me is that I couldn't see the end of the crowd. I think 5'9" is not tall enough to see the end of 800,000 people in one street.

DELANEY TARR: It feels like something out of a book or a movie, to come full circle. Because we took this horrible tragedy, this horrible moment, and we turned it into something more. And I think that that's the most uplifting thing we could have done. And it was a day full of tears, a day full of disorganization and panic and stress, but it was just so worth it. Everything was so worth it. That was the moment that I'll never forget, that none of us will ever forget, because that was something that you can't put into words.

JOHN: We walked through the press line and just did interview after interview after interview, and there were cameras stacked on top of each other. You'd walk two feet and give an interview with one person, and honestly they were all the same questions: "How are you feeling today? What would you want to say to Congress? How many people do you think are here? Who gave you all this money to put this on? How did you guys put this on? If the president was watching, what would you want to say to him?" It was just a whirlwind.

CHRIS GRADY: Too bad the president couldn't make it; he was golfing.

KEVIN TREJOS: Seeing the stage up close, with the Capitol in the background, was so overwhelming. I felt a whole rush of relief. It was surreal: everything we'd been working toward for the past month and a half was here. I remember thinking, *Wow, this is it. This is the future. We're moving on from here. Let's go.*

CHRIS: I didn't check out the stage until the day of, and I just remember being blown away. It was in such a good location, because it had the Capitol Building perfectly in the background.

DYLAN: We were hearing from some news outlets that there were about one million people attending the march in DC. When you're in that crowd, you can't quite fully grasp what that looks like. You can look up a satellite view maybe, see a bunch of streets crowded with random blobs of color. But when you're on that stage, when you look out and see it all? That's something special.

BRENDAN DUFF: Up until that point we had been working out of a tiny office space. It was easy to ignore the good things and only focus on the hate and death threats we were getting. For the students to be able to see the direct impact that they had, that was the most important thing. They could see that people traveled from around the world to be at the DC march. They didn't even have to, because there were marches all over the world. But it was such a surreal experience. The energy backstage was something I don't know if I'll ever feel again in my life.

RYAN: Prior to the start of the march, we got all of the speakers to sit down in a room together and meet. There were people from all over the country, from Los Angeles, from Maryland, from Chicago, from DC, from New York. Everyone was an eloquent speaker and everyone had a prepared speech, which was obviously a little unnerving. Chris Underwood and Naomi Wadler were some of the most intelligent people I've ever met and they were under the age of twelve.

BRADLEY: It was my first time meeting a lot of the other speakers, like Alex King from Chicago and Matt Post from DC. Matt spoke at his high school walkout and he was a senior, and Alex King is a young activist in Chicago. I got to talk to a bunch of kids from Matt's school, a bunch of kids from Chicago. And it was really cool to start to get to know everybody and make connections with that.

SOFIE: There were a lot of other students, like the kids from the National Walkout team who planned the walkout. There were also a bunch of kids from Chicago that we still have relationships with today. People who made that day happen. It was really cool to see how it wasn't just us. The movement had gone way beyond Parkland. It was awesome.

SARAH: We were just kind of warming up to each other, saying hi and stuff, and then we went into a different room, and all the speakers sat in a circle. We did an ice breaker game where we each said our name, where we're from, and a fun fact about ourselves. That's when I met Yolanda King, Martin Luther King Jr.'s granddaughter. I was so excited to meet her, because, like, meeting a King? That's so unbelievable. I never thought I'd meet a King.

MATT DEITSCH: I just felt like my main job that day was to make the survivors feel like celebrities and the celebrities feel like they can relate to the survivors. There was no area for the celebrities to go to be celebrities. If they wanted to have an advantaged viewing, then they had to be clumped in with the people who survived. Not only survived the MSD shooting, but survived the streets of Chicago, survived the streets of DC, survived day-to-day gun violence around the country. And that's why you had someone who was shot in the back and lost the use of her legs in Oakland in her wheelchair next to Kanye West and Kim Kardashian. They had to feel related. We can't keep putting up these walls—we need people to actually relate and feel what the other people are feeling.

RYAN: We wanted to set it up so that someone like Manuel Oliver could have a casual conversation with the Clooneys. I think that added to more of the magic of the march, to have that section up front with all of the MSD students, families, and alumni, and the VIPs. It was sort of like a weird reunion. You'd walk through the crowd and bump into a teacher you had and Steven Spielberg.

SOFIE: It was surreal to be backstage at the march when it finally came to fruition. We'd been working on this since February 15, and then on March 24 all of our work was shown to the world. That was really cool.

BRADLEY: We went through the fences to a big open area for student organizers and other organizers. It was right next to the area reserved for MSD students. We got to stand right next to all the teachers and students who organized locally and who were really integral to helping the movement from home. Some of the organizers of the Parkland march, the walkouts at MSD. The march itself was magical, wonderful, terrifying, stressful, and all at the same time brilliant. There was a loving energy in the air. We were looking around, taking a look at the crowd, and realizing we did this. Which was a completely indescribable feeling.

DANIEL: There was a section at the front of the march specifically for MSD students. We were unified by the tragedy and it was empowering to be among so many people who were as affected by the tragedy as I was. There were other high school groups there and when they saw us coming, they cleared a path, and we chanted as we walked through: *Who are we? MSD!*

CHRIS: I saw a few of my teachers there, which was really cool, including Mr. Foster, who was our AP Gov teacher and also definitely one of the greatest teachers I've ever had. I remember the day of the shooting, he was literally teaching us about interest groups and the NRA when the shooting happened later that day.

SOFIE: There was just so much hope and passion in everyone we saw. And seeing all the Parkland kids on stage . . .

BRENDAN: It was transcendent.

BRADLEY: The first person that came out to talk was Cameron. And Cameron is my sweet little baby sunshine. I'd seen him speak—he's been a huge leader since we started—and do interviews, but him up there was like, we did it. I realized that he did it. I was so proud of him and everyone there. I don't think a single one of us wasn't screaming and clapping the entire time.

SOFIE: When Cameron went up I instantly started crying.

AN EXCERPT FROM CAMERON KASKY'S SPEECH:

To the leaders, skeptics, and cynics who told us to sit down and stay silent, wait your turn. Welcome to the revolution.

It is a powerful and peaceful one because it is of, by, and for the young people of this country. My name is Cameron Kasky. Since this movement began, people have asked me, "Do you think any change is going to come from this?" Look around. We are the change. Everybody here is standing with the future of our society, and for that I thank you.

My generation, having spent our entire lives seeing mass shooting after mass shooting, has learned that our voices are powerful and that our votes matter. We must educate ourselves and start conversations that keep our country moving forward, and we will. We hereby promise to fix the broken system we've been forced into and create a better world for the generations to come. Don't worry, we've got this.

The people in this country now see past the lies. We've seen this narrative before. For the first time, the corrupt aren't controlling our story. We are. The corrupt aren't manipulating the facts. We know the truth. Shooting after shooting, the American

159

people now see one thing they all have in common: the weapons.

Politicians: either represent the people or get out. The people demand a law banning the sale of assault weapons. The people demand we prohibit the sale of high-capacity magazines. The people demand universal background checks. Stand for us or beware: the voters are coming.

On February 14, tragedy struck my hometown and my school, Marjory Stoneman Douglas High. Students lost their lives. Alyssa Alhadeff. Scott Beigel. Martin Duque Anguiano. Aaron Feis. Jaime Guttenberg. Chris Hixon. Luke Hoyer. Cara Loughran. Gina Montalto. Joaquin Oliver. Alaina Petty. Meadow Pollack. Helena Ramsay. Alex Schachter. Carmen Schentrup. Peter Wang. And Nicholas Dworet. All lost their lives in less than seven minutes. And I saved Nicholas for the end because today is Nicholas's birthday. Nicholas, we are all here for you. Happy birthday.

Their families endured great pain. Many others were injured and thousands of young people, my classmates, were forced to become adults, and were targeted as adults. We have to do this for them. We must stand beside those we've lost and fix the world that betrayed them. This doesn't just happen in schools. Americans are being attacked in churches, nightclubs, movie theaters, and on the streets. But we the people can fix this.

For the first time in a long while, I look forward ten years and I feel hope. I see light. I see a system I will be proud of. But it all starts with you. The march is not the climax of this movement, it is the beginning. It is the springboard off of which my generation and all who stand with us will jump into a safer future.

Today is a bad day for tyranny and corruption. Today, we take to the streets in over eight hundred marches around the globe and demand common-sense gun laws. Today is the beginning of a bright new future for this country. And if you think today is good, just wait for tomorrow.

We must protect, educate, and inspire the future, and everybody here is proof that we will do that and the future is looking very bright for this country. Thank you.

DAVID: I wrote my speech thirty minutes before I went to bed the night before, which in hindsight was a very bad idea.

DELANEY: I don't think I started to get nervous until people were like, "Oh yeah, you're speaking, like, third." And I was like, "Oh, okay, cool, I guess." Then we ended up sitting in our little lineup with the chairs, and I was trying to talk to people. I was trying to act as normal as possible, to act like I was not freaking out inside. Because I don't want to give away the fact that I'm nervous. Walking onto the stage was one of those out-of-body experiences, because I did look out to the crowd; I don't remember seeing the crowd, though. It's just blacked out from my memory. The one thing that isn't blacked out was when I put my speech down on the podium and took my hands away, and it immediately flew off the podium and halfway across the stage. I had to chase it down. It was very in character for me. I'm very clumsy, I lose everything, that made sense. Honestly it's the most me moment of that entire speech. I remember somebody cheering out from the crowd, "You're doing great!" and I was like, "Thank you." And I'm not sure if they were laughing at me or with me, but I feel like it was with me because I can't imagine them laughing at me in that moment. It was just a reminder to everybody that I'm a teenager, I'm clumsy, I'm a person. I'm not a presidential figure, I'm not a candidate or anything, I'm just a person.

EXCERPTS FROM DELANEY TARR'S SPEECH:

I'm here for every person who has died at the hands of gun violence, and the many more whose lives were irreparably changed because of it. I hope that that is why we're all here. Because this is more than just a march. This is more than just one day, one event, and then moving on. This is not a mere publicity stunt or a single day in the span of history. This is a movement. This a movement relying on the persistence and passion of its people. We cannot move on. If we move on, the NRA and those against us will win. They want us to forget. They want our voices to be silenced. And they want to retreat into the shadows where they can remain unnoticed. They want to be back on top unquestioned in their corruption. But we cannot—and we will not—let that happen.

Today, and every day, we will continue to fight for those things that are right. We will continue to fight for common sense. We will continue to fight for our lives. We will continue to fight for our dead friends. There will be no faltering, no pauses in our cause. Every moment will be dedicated to those pieces of legislation. Every march, every meeting, every moment.

We are not here for breadcrumbs, we are here for real change. We are here to lead.

The pressure is on for every person in power and it will stay that way. Because they know what is coming. They know that if there is no assault weapons ban passed, then we will vote them out. They know that if there is no tightening of background checks, we will vote them out. They know that if there is no shrinking of magazine capacity we will vote them out. If they continue to ignore us and only pretend to listen, then we will take action where it counts. We will take action in every day and every way until they cannot ignore us anymore. Today, we march, we fight, we roar. We prepare our signs, we raise them high. We know what we want, we know how to get it, and we are not waiting any longer.

MATT: I noticed that my brother was about to go on, so I ran up to the stage. I finally get there, out of breath, right before my brother is about to walk out, and he turns to me and goes, "If they don't boo me, I did it wrong." And I'm like, "What?" And he walks out there and he gives his speech, and in his speech he says that we won't be safe until we arm teachers. And they start booing him.

RYAN: I wrote down three things: my sister's name, because her birthday was February 14, "Arm Teachers," and "Register, Educate, Vote." I had never spoken to such a large crowd before, so I thought about what I like to see from a speaker. They have to look focused, they have to connect with the audience on an individual level. So to do that I actually ended up locking eyes with the guy who found me a job busing tables, my friend Justin. The camera actually cut to him, and you can actually see his facial expression change when I say, "Arm teachers." And you can hear the crowd start to turn. I waited until I heard someone boo, and then I continued, "We need to arm teachers with books, pens, pencils . . ."

EMMA GONZÁLEZ: And then Ryan gets up there and goes, "We need to arm the teachers! We need to arm them!" And he pauses for just the right amount of time. People actually started booing him. And everybody was like, "Wait! What?" Because he didn't tell anybody his plan. He gets up on stage and he says, "We need to arm the teachers!" and everybody's like "Boo!" and he said, "We need to arm them with pens! With pencils! And the money to do their jobs!" And everybody's like, "Yeah!" Oh, it was great! That moment got me.

AN EXCERPT FROM RYAN DEITSCH'S SPEECH:

February 14 is my sister's birthday. She had to spend that birthday huddled under a desk holding Lauren Hogg's, David's sister, her hand. Hoping that she was going to make it home that day. She was premature. She didn't know if she was going to make it at the beginning of her life, and she didn't know if she was going to make it home that day, this year. She might not have stared down the shooter's eyes. She might not have even seen him or known who he was, but he affected her life just as much as everybody else who has spoken on this day.

I know a lot of people are out there saying that we need to make America safe again. And I know that we can't. We cannot make America safe again until we arm our teachers. We need to arm our teachers.

We need to arm them with pencils, pens, paper, and the money they need! They need that money to support their families and to support themselves before they can support the futures and those classrooms! To support the future that sits on that desk waiting to learn. . . . We are done being afraid. We are done being full of fear, because it is a waste of our time. It is not living out what the forefathers envisioned, life, liberty, and the pursuit of happiness. We march today, but this is not over. This is the beginning and from here we fight. It is time to fight for our lives.

RYAN: I followed Miley Cyrus! Hannah Montana! I was like the thirteenth or fourteenth speaker. If I was at an event like that and I knew there were twenty speakers, I'd wait for the performers too, so I had to get their attention. We needed them to feel uncomfortable, so they would actually learn something. It was also fun to see my friends get confused and boo at me.

DANIEL: I work with Ryan as a busboy in a restaurant in Parkland. On one of the TV stations showing the march, they had an interview with me, then they showed Ryan's speech, and then they showed our friend Justin in the crowd, who also worked at the same restaurant. When we got home, the staff told me that they saw us all back-to-back and freaked out. They were so proud of us.

ALEX WIND: Ryan is so clever, and I just loved what he did, in the sense that he really made people listen. That was definitely his intention, and I think he did it so well.

SARAH: Right before my speech, I found out I was going to be going on after Demi Lovato, which is like the most nerve-wracking thing ever, if someone comes up to you and says, "You're going to be speaking after Demi Lovato." I just thought, *Oh, great.* I was so nervous. Then I started reading my speech, and halfway through it, I actually crumpled up my speech, and I threw it over to the side, and just started speaking freestyle, because midway through my speech, I thought to myself, I shouldn't have to read this off a piece of paper. If I really belong here, I should be able to speak this from the heart, so that's exactly what I did.

EMMA: I loved watching all of the, like, people that I had grown so close to in this time period get up there on that stage and speak the way that they did. It was incredible. Like Alex Wind. He was wonderful. And Jackie Corin was screaming! She was killing it! She was legitimately destroying the air in front of her. Like, the air had not one leg to stand on after she was through with it.

BRADLEY: Some of the speeches had this triumphant quality, some were more somber and reflective. I went through this roller coaster of feeling inspired and wonderful and magical and everything is right in the world and we're about to make an incredible change, to instantly plummeting right back down to exactly why we were here in the first place. Realizing that this is for them. Edna Chavez spoke and we chanted her brother Ricardo's name because he had been lost to gun violence. That was really amazing and powerful because it put everything back into perspective. It was a complete roller coaster of emotions.

DANIEL: While they were resetting the stage, they showed onscreen footage of the full crowd, and everyone freaked out. You couldn't even see the end of the crowd down Pennsylvania Ave.

SOFIE: We went on stage during Emma's speech. I had known that Emma was going to do the long moment of silence, but most people didn't know ahead of time. We were all sitting there watching the crowd while she was standing there in silence for multiple minutes. It was crazy to see that the whole world was watching us.

AN EXCERPT FROM EMMA GONZÁLEZ'S SPEECH:

Six minutes, and about twenty seconds. In a little over six minutes, seventeen of our friends were taken from us, fifteen more were injured, and everyone, absolutely everyone in the Douglas community was forever altered. Everyone who was there understands. Everyone who has been touched by the cold grip of gun violence understands. For us, long, tearful, chaotic hours in the scorching afternoon sun were spent not knowing.

No one understood the extent of what had happened. No one could believe that there were bodies in that building waiting to be identified for over a day. No one knew that the people who were missing had stopped breathing long before any of us had even known that a code red had been called. No one could comprehend the devastating aftermath, or how far this would reach, or where this would go.

For those who still can't comprehend, because they refuse to, I'll tell you where it went. Six feet into the ground, six feet deep. Six minutes and twenty seconds with an AR-15, and my friend Carmen would never complain to me about piano practice. Aaron Feis would never call Kyrah "miss sunshine," Alex Schachter would never walk into school with his brother Ryan, Scott Beigel would never joke around with Cameron at camp, Helena Ramsay would never hang around after school with Max, Gina Montalto would never wave to her friend Liam at lunch, Joaquin Oliver would never play basketball with Sam or Dylan. Alaina Petty would never, Cara Loughran would never, Chris Hixon would never, Luke Hoyer would never, Martin Duque Anguiano would never, Peter Wang would never, Alyssa Alhadeff would never, Jaime Guttenberg would never, Meadow Pollack would never.

[EXTENDED MOMENT OF SILENCE]

Since the time that I came out here, it has been six minutes and twenty seconds. The shooter has ceased shooting and will soon abandon his rifle, blend in with the students as they escape, and walk free for an hour before arrest. Fight for your lives before it's someone else's job.

MATT: The silence wasn't on the paper. I didn't know it was going to happen. I was talking to Emma and Emma was crying just on the side of the stage, and I thought she was so nervous, so I give her a hug and try to hype her up. And she goes up there like a badass, struts out there and starts her speech, and then she goes silent. I had no idea what was going on.

EMMA: I knew what I was going to do for my speech a while beforehand. I was working on it for a while. I knew that I was going to have the silence. I knew it was going to make it easier for me to write it, because I knew that if I had a silence I wouldn't have to write anything for that gap. But I would still be on stage for a specific amount of time. I knew what I was doing, but not a lot of people did. I think I only told two people. I asked Sarah, like, "Hey, how do you think this sounds, I need an opinion, I've kept this to myself for too long, what if it's bad?"

I thought, okay, if I'm going last, I need to reiterate why we're here. And I need to enforce how we feel. I need to capitalize off of the impact that the speech is going to have. And I need to make that impact as large as possible because I know how far-reaching it's going to be.

SARAH: She ended it with "Fight with your lives before someone else has to," and the crowd just erupted. It was such a wild moment. It still feels like it wasn't real.

DYLAN: We're just going to breeze over what it was like on that stage during Emma González's speech. We're not going to talk about that. Incredible. I'm still recovering.

SOFIE: During Alex Wind's speech, he went off. I've never seen such passion in that boy in my life. I remember grabbing Brendan and saying, "Alex is a politician!" Alex is one of our best friends, and watching him speak in front of all those people, knowing what a goof he is in real life, was crazy. When he said things like, "What are we going to do, arm Mickey Mouse at Disney World?" I thought, *Wow*. I would never have thought that this is what our lives would be.

BRENDAN: He was just yelling. I've never seen him like that. I was so proud. I remember Sofie turning to me and going, "That's Alex Wind!"

SOFIE: That's our Alex!

ALEX: It was really cold, so I don't know if I was shaking from the cold or from nerves. There were a lot of people from Douglas actually sitting on stage at the march. One of my closest friends was up there, and right before I went on stage I pointed at him and I made eye contact. It was really important having so many familiar faces there and knowing that I had so many friends in the audience and backstage supporting me—that was a comforting feeling.

RYAN: The most powerful moment in the march for me was Alex Wind's speech. I had heard it before because a lot of people were practicing the night before in our hotel rooms, so I knew what he was going to say but I didn't know how he would say it. The last line is something like "It's a battle of life and death, and we choose life." After he said that, I saw a young African American girl put her fist up in the crowd in solidarity. This was a girl who didn't go to MSD; we didn't know her, she didn't know us. She and Alex didn't know each other, but they shared that moment, alongside hundreds of thousands of people. It felt like a message of hope. Just another thing that shows me that we're doing the right thing, that we're on the right side of hope.

AN EXCERPT FROM ALEX WIND'S SPEECH:

In the wake of the tragedy on February 14, we as students, as youths, decided that if adults were not going to take action, we would. No gun-related legislation has been passed in this country since 2008, ten years ago. Since 2008 there have been at least ninety-five mass shootings in this country . . . senseless violence in the cities of our nation and cities like Miami, Chicago, and Baltimore. It needs to stop.

People believe that the youth of this country are insignificant; people believe that the youth have no voice. When Joan of Arc fought back the English forces she was seventeen years old. When Mozart wrote his first symphony he was eight years old. To those people that tell us that teenagers can't do anything, I say that we were the only people that could have made this movement possible.

Together, we will use our voices to make sure that our schools, churches, movie theaters, and concerts, and our streets become safer without having them feel like prisons. If teachers start packing heat, are they going to arm pastors, ministers, and rabbis? Are they going to arm the guys scanning tickets at the movie theater? Are they going to arm the person wearing the Mickey costume at Disney? This is what the National Rifle Association wants and we will not stand for it.

We would not need metal detectors and clear backpacks and more weapons in our streets if there weren't weapons of war in the hands of civilians.

For too long our government has been useless on this issue. Our job as their constituents is to make sure we know what they are thinking. There are over 250 representatives that have not come out with a public stance on this issue. It is our job to make sure that we call them up and force them out of the shadow of corruption and into the light of justice.

As teens, people think we don't like to wait around for things, and they are sometimes right. A lot of you are probably wondering, what now? Now we need to come together on all fronts and push aside those that divide us. Now we need to get on the phone and call representatives and push them to stop incumbency and take action. Now we need to educate ourselves on which politicians are truly working for the people, and *which ones we want to vote out. Because at the end of the day, bullets do not discriminate, so why should we?*

It is not about your race, it is not about your sexual orientation, it is not about your ethnicity, it is not about your gender, it is not about where you live, or how much money you make, and it most certainly is not about political parties. All it comes down to is life or death.

To all the politicians out there, if you take money from the NRA, you have chosen death. If you have not expressed your constituents' public stance on this issue, you have chosen death. If you do not stand with us by saying we need to pass commonsense gun legislation you have chosen death. And none of the millions of people marching in this country today will stop until they see those against us out of office because we choose life.

JACLYN: A few days before the march, some friends and I found a video of Reverend Martin Luther King's granddaughter, Yolanda Renee King. She was leading a chant in front of a large crowd at nine years old. Her words were even more uplifting. She was incredibly well-spoken for her age. It was in watching that video that I knew she needed to be on that stage. The night before, I was frantically trying to set it up, and the next morning we got her to the building where we were getting ready and

I spent the whole morning with Yolanda. No one knew that it was going to happen; no one knew that I was going to bring her out on stage. I was so excited because I knew everyone was going to go crazy. She was the sweetest girl, and her parents, her mom and MLK III, were so kind. It was an absolute honor to be in their presence; they carry a legacy that is unlike any other. I spoke toward the end of the march, and there were almost a million people out there, and the thing that we had been working toward day in and day out for almost a month was actually here.

Finally, it was my turn to speak. I felt my nerves racing throughout my body. I was terrified because we were in a large crowd where a dangerous incident could easily present itself. I forced myself to be brave, though—I had to remember why I was there. I got more comfortable when I saw the people in the front that I knew, because the front section of the march was the Parkland community. I saw a poster of Joaquin Oliver, one of the victims, and I just got angry because I knew why his face was on that poster and I knew why all these people were gathering, and all the emotions just filled in my body and I just got really mad and confident on the stage.

EMMA: My favorite moment of the whole day was when Jackie was on stage and said, "And before I leave, I have a very special guest." And she goes over and she brings Yolanda King out, and Yolanda starts cheering and stuff and doing her chants. It was the best moment. That was legitimately word for word what Martin Luther King Jr. said: *I have a dream that one day little black girls will be holding hands with little white girls.* Jackie's a little white girl. I'm gonna say it for the record, Jackie's a little white girl. And she and Yolanda King holding hands and chanting together was incredible. I don't care if that wasn't specifically about gun violence in that moment. It was about empowerment. And that's kind of what the march was about too.

JACLYN: After my speech, I brought Yolanda out and I swear to god the second she said, "I'm Yolanda King, the granddaughter of . . ." when she said granddaughter, the crowd went crazy and she was squeezing my hand so tight. It was a really beautiful moment. She just really made the difference in the march. She really showed how history repeats itself, unfortunately, because tragedy always incites change. She filled the crowd with hope.

AN EXCERPT FROM JACLYN CORIN'S SPEECH:

My name is Jaclyn Corin, and I am proud to say that Parkland is my home. Parkland is the heart of this movement, but just as a heart needs blood to pump, my hometown needs the alliance of other communities to properly spread this message.

We openly recognize that we are privileged individuals and would not have received as much attention if it were not for the affluence of our city. Because of that, however, we share the stage today and forever with those who have always stared down the barrel of a gun. This issue is undoubtedly an epidemic that affects communities of all classes, an epidemic that the Center for Disease Control does not have the funds to research. This disease continues to spread, even though we have discovered the cure. But our government officials closed their ears because it involves change. A change that does not align with their own agenda.

That is why Parkland cannot and will not do this alone. There is strength in numbers, and we need each and every one of you to keep screaming at your own congressman. Don't be scared just because they have Senator in front of their name. Our elected officials have seen American after American drop from a bullet, and instead of waking up to protect us they have been hitting the snooze button. But we're here to shake them awake.

Each congressman has a local office in their district, so pay them a visit or organize a Town Hall. They will be home for the next two weeks for congressional recess. Have them hear you out, because they work for us. And if they still won't meet with you, remind them that you invited their opponent, because we all know *they'll show up then. We cannot keep America great if we cannot keep America safe. And ninety-six deaths by firearms every day is not what I would call great.*

Our First Amendment right is our weapon of war in this, a weapon that should be on our streets, a weapon that cannot kill but can heal. Love will always outweigh the hate, as the universe is on the side of justice.

So I need each and every one of you no matter your age to continue the fight alongside us, because hearts cannot pump without blood and I don't want your community to join the ghastly inner circle that mine is now part of.

In the end, we are all fighting for our lives. But we are a great generation and will be the ones to make America safe.

ALEX: A lot of the people from outside of Florida, those speakers made such an impact. Matt Post, Trevon Bosley, and D'Angelo McDade and Alex King did such a good job of showing the other side of gun violence and showed the crowd how we all can come together despite our different experiences.

DYLAN: Each and every speaker at the march sat together backstage in one section oozing with nerves, anxiety, and excitement; walking over to that area, you felt this wave of motivation and drive. It was like getting punched in the face by the physical embodiment of every single inspiring TED Talk out there.

KYRAH SIMON: The march wasn't as big a symbol for me as it was for other people in the organization. I just knew I had to go and witness it. I don't think I was negative about the march itself, but things that happened at the march did upset me. I felt like after the shooting, things immediately became very political and people lost sight of the humanity of it all. Those were children, fathers, brothers, sisters that died that day. I didn't like how it became a gun reform versus no gun reform conversation. It was presented as two sides of the spectrum when really this was an issue that should've united everybody. It made me upset and resentful at the time, but I've worked past that and I'm over it now. When you grow as a person and develop some maturity you realize you can't just walk around mad and angry all the time. I can't be mad at people, at other human beings, and villainize them because I feel differently from them.

DAVID: One mistake that I think we really made, that I really made, is the fact that I didn't say, "These are ten policies we need to go after." That was what we needed to do, but I failed to do so. We need people to go out and register people to vote and we need people to go out and canvass and talk to people about gun policy.

KYRAH: At that moment in my life, I had a lot of negative feelings toward March for Our Lives, because I felt like they were speaking for people they shouldn't speak for. Most of those sentiments stemmed from my own personal anger. I was angry the day of the march, but I was directing it toward the wrong people. I had a lot of misplaced anger over Helena's death. My anger dissipated in the months following the march because I realized that holding anger in my heart only weighs me down and makes you a negative, disgusting person. When your heart is ugly, you're ugly. I'm still coming to terms with the fact that the shooting is real and it happened and my friend is not alive. Everyone that died that day is gone, and even though I can't understand why it happened and how it happened, it happened. I'm still coming to terms with that.

JOHN: At the end, the stage manager told us all to go on. And we didn't know what we were doing; we just knew this was the finale. We were chanting "We want change" and hearing hundreds of thousands of people chanting with us. We were literally shaking Capitol Hill. We were shaking DC. Your voice may be small, but when you are part of this big collective that believes in the same thing you do and you put all your voices together, that's when you can actually create permanent, substantial change. I'm so humbled to be a part of this movement and that march from the beginning. When we were all up there chanting "We want change," I'll never forget that moment.

DYLAN: Being there before the speeches, though, was absolutely nothing compared to being there after. The constant sense of anticipation and excitement that had permeated the air was instantly replaced by a new and refreshing sense of relief and love. This movement is so much more than a bunch of dumb teens screaming into a microphone. This is a community. This is our community. We are all in this together. Not one of us could've done anything without the help of each and every supporter.

RYAN: Eight hundred eighty marches around the world, marches on every continent. For one moment on this earth, everyone was standing and saying the same thing. It was an amazing feat. That day people showed that they cared.

ADAM ALHANTI: What I took out of the march was that it was about what's next. It was about thinking about the next day. It wasn't about being there in the moment for me. I think most people forget to grasp that—we're focusing on what's right in front of us. I was thinking about how it was great that we did a march on Washington, but were the people in the Capitol listening? I hope so, but I don't know. The experience for me was about doing more than standing on the street. Before, I was thinking, we're going to march and it will be great and they'll listen. But when it happened, I thought, *This isn't enough. We need to do more.*

DAVID: The biggest thing to realize is that unless every single one of those people votes, it doesn't matter. Unless we don't constantly fight for change, we're never going to get it. You can't just show up and march; you have to get out and fucking vote. You have to go out and be a delegate and go out and make active change; you have to run for office and be that change. Because the people that we have right now are people that have been there so long that they've learned the methods of constantly getting into office and doing jack shit. Unless we hold our elected officials responsible and unless we educate ourselves on who we're voting for and how, we're never going to be able to create this change. For our children and for our future.

CAMERON KASKY: I just have to hope that everybody who showed up that day will vote. Protest is patriotic. Getting out there and demanding more from our country is one of the best things you can do for yourself, but voting is the most important thing.

DELANEY: It was so surreal. And probably one of the best days of my life. I know that being on that stage at the end and having everybody singing together and standing together—even talking about it now I get chills. Because it's one of those things that you can never imagine would happen, but was legitimately probably the best moment of my life. That was definitely a peak, right there. You're standing in front of 800,000 people, Jennifer

Hudson is belting out in front of everyone, and you're standing behind her, and you know that people are there for what you stand for. People are there because they care. They're not there for these performers, they're there to see the students. That's insane. To have 800,000 people come in DC alone, and to have almost two million people across the country come because they agree with something that a group of teenagers is saying. That a group of teenagers is just trying to get people to care about. And it worked. It genuinely worked.

DANIEL: I felt a lot of pride that day. Those are my friends on stage. I was so proud of them for putting this together, how hard they worked. It was amazing seeing everyone in "activist mode." These were regular high schoolers who were worried about their GPA and now they are on stage, on television in front of millions of people, creating a global movement. They were inspiring. Welcome to the revolution.

JOHN: After the march happened, we were still backstage as the crowd slowly started to disperse. We went back to the main building, and this time as we were walking by, things had completely switched from before. People knew who we were. People knew we were the Parkland kids, but after the march, people started walking up to us, yelling "hi" and screaming so that we could give them our attention. But I'm just a kid from Parkland, and them being at that march and thinking the same thing and feeling the way we all feel, they are literally me. All these high schoolers, all these kids, all these adults are just like me. It gave a weird celebrity aspect to it—these people trying to get our attention, saying, "Oh my gosh, I love you." That's strange to me because they have the power to do that too. I was just given this opportunity because of this unfortunate tragedy that happened at my school. That somehow gave a platform to the kids who are part of this movement. But they have the same platforms as us, the same audience; they just need to speak their mind, and never give up, and be persistent.

ADAM: Most people would say the march was powerful, or inspirational. But I think it was more like the end of a chapter. It was like this period of grief that we all had for a month, pure grief—we're still grieving, but that was pure sadness—and the march sealed that up. It was no longer just tears—we were doing the right thing for those seventeen people and the thousands more who have lost their lives.

SOFIE: After the march, we all reconvened at the hotel and had a mini party. That was the first moment since everything where we got to look back and not necessarily look forward. By March 25 we were already planning other stuff. But that night we got to just take it in and be together.

EMMA: What I loved the most about the day of the march was the party that we had in Matt and Ryan's hotel room that night after the march. We went and got food and then hung out, like, all twenty-five of us were chilling. Alex Wind was doing a talent show, and he was a fantastic MC. He would say things like, "Sofie Whitney is going to sing the alphabet backward. Sarah Chadwick is going to put her whole fist in her mouth. John Barnitt is going to portray his new character, Helja the Hippo!" who was basically a mom with this crazy Boston accent, who would talk about how overpriced groceries are nowadays, and how hard it is to get up stairs. It was just priceless.

ALEX: We were just unwinding and it was a fun thing that I thought of to do. Let me just make up a random talent for someone to do on the spot and watch them figure out how to do it. It wasn't like it was going to be the craziest thing they had to do that day.

EMMA: Alex was just so good at pulling things from nowhere and making people do them.

ALFONSO: My talent was bringing everybody food. I ordered Johnny Rockets—onion rings and cheese fries. They were gone before I got back to them.

BRENDAN: That was the best part: celebrating everyone's accomplishments. There are a lot of people in this movement who aren't front and center but are doing work all the time. So to know that every single person played a part in making this all happen was so cool.

MATT: After the march, I was walking around DC with Brad, and we were talking to everyone who had participated. I talked to probably 1,500 people in the next two hours, just quick conversations about how everything was happening. They had no idea who I was and it was just awesome to hear them say, "Yeah, my eight-year-old brought me here and told me that this meant something to her" or "My fifteen-year old son brought us and told us this was important." It was the most incredible thing I'd ever seen. I had grandparents come up to me and say, "I marched out here with Martin Luther King and this had the same energy that that day had, and you could feel the change in the air."

JOHN: Even when you're little, people tell you that you can accomplish anything if you put your mind to it or if you work hard enough, but deep down we know we're just one small, little piece in this whole entire world. You think that no one is going to care about you, you're not going to be the person who makes an impact. It's going to be the person next to you or the person in a different state or country. What we learned from the situation was to get out and take that grieving and completely switch that to motivation. To know what you want, to show the nation that yes, we're teenagers, but we know what we're talking about and we can create change if you're not going to help us. These kids that were struggling to get an A in Algebra II, these kids that were stressed out about their teachers, and the SATs, and what they were going to wear to prom, those kids were able to accomplish so much in so little time with so much trauma that has happened to them. When people say, "Anything is possible if you put your mind to it" or "Hard work pays off," all of those cheesy and overused sayings, they say it because it's true.

CAMERON: The march was exactly what I expected it to be. It was a great event; it was beautiful. There was a spirit there, and that spirit is what inspired our current project Road to Change. That spirit was about everyone just wanting to do better. The march was our way of showing America that we want to do better, and we can. America is a country that is fueled by boundless dreams and small victories. We all overcome things together. We dare ourselves to move forward; we dare ourselves to do better. We push ourselves into the future, and together we say that even if this isn't easy, we owe it to our people as the greatest country in the world to make this change.

ALEX: It's almost as if the march was the end of chapter one and now we're starting chapter two. The day of the march was insane. It was so surreal. It was all of our hard work finally culminating in this major peak. And we have to find a way to build on that peak, which I think we're doing with Road to Change.

MATT: I sat down on the Capitol lawn and just lay down because I was dead exhausted and I was looking up at the sky. And I looked over at Bradley and he just had this huge smile on his face, and I said, "Brad, we have so much work to do."

Jammal Lemy

A VIEW FROM THE CROWD: MARCH 24

ON SATURDAY, MARCH 24, Jammal Lemy, a graduate of Marjory Stoneman Douglas, stood near the front of a sea of hundreds of thousands of people at the March for Our Lives, one of the largest protests in American history. He stood alongside other MSD students and members of Manuel Oliver's organization, Change the Ref, as they held a banner honoring Joaquin Oliver, Jammal's friend and Manuel's son. Jammal's experience in the crowd that day propelled him to use his creative talents to get involved in the March for Our Lives movement.

I'm the creative director for March for Our Lives. While I wasn't formally involved in the earliest days of planning, my involvement in and dedication to the movement have been serious since the jump.

Before any of this happened, my friend and classmate Matt Deitsch and I were designing T-shirts for this line we created called War & Peace. It was a juxtaposition where the War T-shirt had a cool intricate flower patch in the background and the Peace T-shirt had a bomber plane bombing a city, so it was a visual demonstrating the effects of war. Matt and I got close working together on this. We were planning to donate the proceeds from the line to microfund projects within war-stricken areas. For instance, if a school or community center needed resources to finish their project, we would donate X amount of dollars.

Matt and I were at a time in our lives when we wanted to see where we could put our creative talents to use. My father had always educated me about human right issues and how to be an empathetic human being. I feel that I have a moral obligation to use my god-given set of skills to make the world a better place, and I knew that making T-shirts and microfunding projects with the profits would do exactly that. Moving toward our final production plan and rollout, I was anxious and super excited. I don't think I ever wanted to get anything off the ground more than I wanted to make War & Peace succeed.

Joaquin Oliver was kind of like an intern for me. I had a creative company that I had just started, Mal3times, and Joaquin offered that if I needed any help he would be there for me. I was working really hard to get things started and it meant a lot to me that he offered to help out. We had planned a photoshoot for that Friday, February 16, and Joaquin was going to be the model for it. Then tragedy happened on Wednesday, and Joaquin was one of those killed. That's a reality I have to live with every day. I think I work so hard with MFOL to make sure no one ever has to go through what we here in Parkland had to go through.

After the shooting, it seemed as if time stood still and everything happening outside of Broward County didn't matter. I lost one of my close friends and everything was just going crazy—things were happening so fast. All I can remember is how many people around the world offered their support. After previous school shootings happened, the last thing on my mind was to take action and fight the people who, as I now realize, have constantly dropped the ball, leaving room for massacres like what happened at Douglas.

But nonetheless, people like the ones who would later become some of my friends felt the need to speak out and make their voices heard. This movement was really starting to happen, and Matt was really involved and encouraging me to be involved as well, but I really needed time to take everything in. I can distinctly remember Matt coming over to pick up a shirt I had made that said STOP GUN VIOLENCE, the one he would eventually wear on a panel with Steve Kerr. I just recall him telling me how impactful this movement would be, but I guess my pessimism about the system had left no hope in my heart. And at the time, it didn't feel completely ethical to me. People were still grieving, and at first I wasn't sure if it felt right to take it to the national stage and push an agenda.

About a week before the march, when things were really

getting amped up, all of the founders were flying everywhere and doing all of this press. Matt was flying around the country and he was super busy, but at the same time he was still really encouraging me to be a part of what they were doing. I was impressed with what they were putting together and the response they were getting, but I still wasn't sure I would be able to go down to DC early for the march. But something inside me kept pushing me to explore and find out more. Have you ever had an urge to do something but you can't seem to understand why? That is exactly how I felt the week before the march. I was told by many people that it would be like nothing we could have ever imagined. I emailed Matt asking for a press pass, hoping to get some behind-the-scenes footage. His response was "you'd experience the march better from the crowd." At the moment, I personally didn't know how to feel, but I took his word for it. I tried to figure out how to get myself there.

There was a group of people who were working together with Manuel Oliver, Joaquin's dad, called Real Man to Man Action. I had designed a shirt for Manuel's organization, Change the Ref. And someone from the group said that since I had designed the shirt, I should be compensated for my work, and he offered to buy me a ticket to the march. At this point it was the day before the march. Later, he hit me up and told me that sending me to the march was the best money he ever spent. And it's true, because that ticket ultimately changed my life.

The amount of love and camaraderie that I felt that weekend

was pretty much indescribable. I get chills now thinking about it. You could see it all over the city. That weekend you could just feel it in the air, it was electric. Even though we were all still grieving, it was so cool to see how people came together. It was an amaz ing feeling being surrounded by friends.

On the day of the march, being out there with everyone, I'd never seen that many people in my life. It was just a sea of people. Every news outlet had a different random number, but I promise you there were definitely a million people. Everyone was there: celebrities, moms from Iowa, anybody you can think of was there. I saw ninety-year-olds marching, little kids march- ing. It was so powerful to see all the kids there because given the size of the event and the security issues, it meant a lot that parents brought these little kids out to witness it.

We started out in the crowd walking along with everyone else, and then at one point, the crowd started pushing all of the MSD kids to the front. I mean, it literally parted like the Red Sea to let us through. The whole time, the crowd was just cheering and supporting us and waving their signs. I had my camera with me and I couldn't stop taking pictures. The creativity was out of this world. I was with Change the Ref and we eventually ended up in front in the VIP section. We hung up a banner of Manuel's that had Joaquin's face on it. We stood there for hours. The whole day sort of felt like an out-of-body experience, because no one could've imagined the way it unfolded or understood the scope of it.

I'm normally not an emotionally reactive person, but at the march, I couldn't manage to keep my composure. Being side-by-side with Manny showed me where Joaquin got his outgoing personality from. Change the Ref brought an extremely large banner for the helicopter shot, and even though my arms were tired, I wouldn't have wanted to share the experience with anyone else. Since then Manuel, Joaquin's mom, Patricia, and I have grown pretty close. I can't forget my little sister Victoria Gonzalez, Joaquin's girlfriend.

After the speakers and the performances, we wandered through the streets and ended up running into a group of mothers who had lost their children to gun violence. They wanted to thank us for what we were doing. Everyone that we met on the streets of DC was just so friendly and warm. That weekend felt like the embodiment of love and unification. It felt insane to have such a huge, massive march like that and not see a single counter-protester or any opposition. To see people from all walks of life coming out to support us like this was just overwhelming. Young, old, black, white, everyone came together because this issue affected them too. It wasn't something we had to handle alone.

It's surprising because in this day and age, I never would've expected to see people come together like that. It made us realize that the next steps of the movement, Road to Change, could actually work and people might actually support it.

In the beginning, I had been pretty unsure about participating in the march and the movement. But now I realize that I didn't understand the purpose or see where it could go at first. But at the march, it all clicked for me in that moment. Joaquin and a lot of the victims—they were kids. And it's crazy to think about how quickly their lives were taken and how quickly America can just move on. This is why the young people needed their voices to be heard. They need to keep talking so people will listen.

March for Our Lives officially offered me the task of designing merch, and I was genuinely excited. Aside from creative expression, designing for a good cause is something all creatives can agree with. They came to me saying that we have to attack the NRA where it hurts. The NRA's main defense is patriotism, and we can take that away from them by designing merch that is just as patriotic.

At first I didn't agree and thought we should ride our own wave; but Matt insisted. I pulled an all-nighter trying to come up with a design that could change the world. I thought to myself and wondered if anyone tried putting a QR code on clothes. A lot of what I had already had the American flag incorporated, so the QR code made its way on the flag. After spending all night designing, I sent the final to Matt and then passed out. The next morning, I had a bunch of texts from Matt saying that this shirt could win us the election. Moving forward in society, most of our phone cameras have QR readers already integrated in. So, imagine being able to register everyone around you in two minutes or less? When you take a photo of the shirt, it automatically pulls up the voter registration page on the MFOL website. We've already registered thousands of people and hope to register thousands more with a combination of innovation and fashion.

Ever since I've taken real interest in creative work, I know my skills would be most useful helping the world, not only the world directly around me. Art is the most effective medium to convey messages, in my opinion. Along with the T-shirts and sweatshirts with the QR code that I'm so proud of, I now can say I have a major role in all of the content that is released to the public on behalf of MFOL. I wear many hats, handling video production, designing, speaking on panels, and then handling marketing strategies. I want to touch as many hearts as possible, in any creative manner. I know it's our duty as the youth of America to never stay quiet. And we won't.

Matt Deitsch

MOBILIZING COUNTRYWIDE AND THE FUTURE OF THE MOVEMENT: APRIL AND BEYOND

THE MARCH FOR OUR LIVES was a history-making event that expanded and energized the conversation around tighter gun laws in America. But the organizers of March for Our Lives were looking beyond the march, determined to help people around the country turn that conversation into action. So Marjory Stoneman Douglas alum Matt Deitsch helped launch Road to Change, a cross-country tour to get young people educated, registered, and motivated to vote.

I have been to too many funerals for children. The sight of someone younger than myself in a casket will never leave my memory, permanently etched as a reminder of what we are truly fighting for.

No more.

No more senseless violence taking the lives of innocent people in a school, movie theater, church, concert, workplace, or at home. Parkland was the safest city in Florida for nearly a decade, and then seventeen people lost their lives. The idea of safety is simply that, an idea.

Calling America the land of opportunity seems like false advertising when children are being shot and killed every single day. Those in political office taking money from the NRA openly block policies to combat the gun violence epidemic. The gun manufacturers who give commission to the NRA are blocking regulations in the name of profit. These regulations would save lives. The politicians that send thoughts and prayers, and only thoughts and prayers, are not fighting for the lives of their constituents, they are only thinking of themselves. These selfish political puppets are perpetuating the problems plaguing our nation.

How do you put an end to violence that allows individuals in power to profit? You organize. More people want to live than want to profit. More people want to save their neighbor than oppress their neighbor. More people want peace than war—but there are powerful people who prefer wealth to peace.

Organizing put an end to the war in Vietnam. Young people organized to stop their friends from coming back in body bags. Today, the war is on our soil, with our weapons, taking our lives. It will take young people organizing to end this war too.

We have access to educational tools that our founding fathers could not imagine. Around the country, I have met ten-year-olds who know policy better than five-term congressmen.

As a film student, I did not have a grasp on gun policy before the shooting occurred. Then I studied and was able to become an expert, informing politicians and other young people on the reality in our country. I have seen many forms of gun violence across the United States and they all need to be addressed by the leadership of this great nation.

Our politicians do not lead, they respond slowly and sheepishly. They give excuses, not solutions. But we have the capacity to organize and educate at a rate the world has never seen. This generation has lived with mass shootings becoming normalized while simultaneously having every question answered with multiple sources. We live in a more connected yet detached reality. That is why the young people of this world can see this system we have inherited and create a unified front for change. We deserve a system that fights for us, not a system we constantly have to fight.

Following the Town Hall that we organized on CNN, my brother came up to me and said we were going to go to Congress. We reached out to our congressman and local representatives, who assisted us in booking the meetings we wanted with everyone from the majority whip to the speaker of the house. We secured nearly two hundred face-to-face meetings with people in Congress because we understood that each and every politician would love a photo with the Parkland students. We knew they wanted to push these pictures through their campaign donor emails, to pitch themselves as human beings to their constituents. The day of our meetings, I made the demand—no press, no photos. We forced these elected officials to sit in a room with up to fifteen students and hear everything we had to say—we learned who these people really were.

Our country is currently run by an incredibly out of touch group of people who listen to the biggest donors and rarely their constituents. When we visited their offices, most of them needed staff members (usually much younger than they are) to answer the simplest questions. Remember, these meetings occurred within a few weeks of the shooting and none of us had a vast knowledge of gun violence policy, so the fact that these politicians still knew less was deeply disturbing.

Some of the politicians snuck photos and posted them on social media despite our request. House Speaker Paul Ryan had maybe ten cameras outside of his office trying to get in, and he snuck a photo (lying about the content of our meeting in his Twitter caption). These politicians care more about optics than their constituents.

That is why we made it our mission at March for Our Lives to actually listen, learn, and build with the most vulnerable people in our nation. In order to truly improve the status quo that allows for the death of children to be ignored, we must understand the reality of what is happening in America day to day. Ignoring the suffering of our most vulnerable perpetuates the problems. The interest that comes from inaction creates more suffering when morally just leaders could solve these problems.

When congressmen lie about the words within our constitution (as they have done to us) then it's time to elect people who took US history and government courses this century. The young people of America have begun coming together at a rate we have never seen before. The youth will fix this great nation and truly lead us to a more compassionate future. We can only do this together and with love.

When we were organizing for the march we would repeat "March twenty-fourth" over and over again, constantly referring to it as a generational event (even before raising a single cent). We spoke the success of that day into existence. My focus was on the march, but for me it wasn't just about making it better, it was about coordinating with the adults we were bringing in. I thought it was important that any adult who wanted to work for us needed to have a point person that was a kid within the organization. We felt like, if we didn't know everything that was going on, then it wouldn't be handled the right way. It wasn't that we didn't trust these adults; it's just that they had no idea what they were doing in regards to the message we were trying to convey.

What we were trying to do was so different from what other organizations do. Other organizations build something in a structure meant to stand the test of time, similar to the way the NRA is built—but we don't want the March for Our Lives to exist, we want this organization to complete a mission and render itself obsolete. Other large-scale gun violence prevention groups told us a march would not be a powerful statement. Of course our answer to that was, "Well, we think it will."

Still, we were worried about turnout. We originally thought there were going to be ninety people at the march. That was our first estimate. My reasoning was that Jaclyn Corin had gotten a hundred people to go to Tallahassee and DC is much farther. Still, we did everything we could to make the march the biggest event possible, and we ended up with millions of people attending marches around the country. But we weren't really looking past that day.

We were trying to pass laws that this Congress won't even look at, and we knew that March 24 wasn't going be to the entire battle. So my job from that moment on was to think about what we were going to do after the march. Our Road to Change tours came from those meetings. The fundraising we were able to do for other gun violence groups came from those meetings. We created coalitions to raise tens of thousands for groups on the ground in communities actively saving lives.

Road to Change was inspired by the farmers' movement in California and the Freedom Riders. In order to topple corruption we must organize and educate—we also must listen to and learn from every community in this great nation. The tour began as a way to register new voters to create an educated voting force, but as young leaders from Chicago, St. Louis, Milwaukee, and tons of other stops joined the tour, its scope grew much wider. It became a personified meeting of the two Americas. The compassionate America and the uninformed America. We learned that this issue is not polarizing. We are empowering young people, who are better connected now than at any time in American history, to be the leaders in their community.

If we don't foster leadership within community structures by going place to place and inspiring people to stand up before atrocities happen to them, then we fail, and America isn't America anymore. America was founded on the values of life, liberty, and the pursuit of happiness. Those very principles are what we have to fight for.

We can't allow our representatives to be hypocrites when they say "Stand up for the constitution." For example, when we were in Iowa, a group of about fifty of us, mostly local students age ten to twenty, went to Representative Steve King's office. We announced two days earlier that we were going, we called and left a message, and we sent an email to a scheduler who never got back to us.

When we got to his office, there was one woman there, and she told us, "I'm not here to talk about personal attacks." And yet, we argued, Steve King had attacked Emma González on Facebook. She answered with, "I can't defend that. That's the campaign, not Steve King or his office. I'm here to talk about policy."

A ten-year-old boy named Langston from Iowa City stood up and said, "I want to ask about universal background checks, because even the conservatives I know want universal background checks. But Steve King has openly spoken out against it. What do you think we can do about that?"

Her response was, "I don't want to talk about policy."

She had security remove us from the office, and they didn't allow photos or press, so I took out the copy of the constitution I had in my pocket. I read the first amendment: freedom of the press, which they obstructed; freedom to peaceably assemble, which they tried repeatedly to break up; and freedom of speech, which they undermined by censoring our ability to communicate with our representative.

When kids grow up and are able to vote, I want them to remember who is standing in the way of the constitution, and it is not groups of students gathering. It is their representatives and it is Congress.

Most of that conversation at Steve King's office was led by thirteen- and fourteen-year-olds from Iowa. And meetings like that have been happening all over the country. I feel like a big part of what we accomplished on the tour is creating a handbook for what leadership should look like in this country.

We put ourselves on the front lines so that other students don't have to be afraid to. We receive threats from people all the time, especially people saying that they'd shoot us if they saw us.

That's why we're doing this. Not to take everyone's guns—our policy is to leave law-abiding gun owners alone. But if you're willing to threaten someone for trying to save lives, maybe you shouldn't have a gun.

I feel like much of what is shared with the public is news that Cameron Kasky's house or David Hogg's house gets SWAT'ed, and that our lives are at risk. But our lives are at risk regardless of whether we speak out or don't. Cameron, my brother, my sister, could've all been killed on February 14. Countless kids could've been killed in any of the school shootings that have happened since. When we meet young leaders like Alex King and Arieyanna Williams from Chicago, Bria Smith from Milwaukee, Ramon Contreras from Harlem, young people who have seen intense gun violence their entire lives—we know we must come together and use all of our strengths to overcome this constant threat on innocent life.

If I could sit down with every single American in this country and talk about this issue, from everyone in Bismarck, North Dakota, to everyone in Congress, to everyone in Ocala, Florida— everyone who disagrees with us—I think we could work together to find solutions and solve this easily. But, like we found in Steve King's office in Iowa, people often don't want to have this conversation. People don't want to talk about the fact that 80 percent of the world's gun violence (and 86 percent of women killed in gun violence) occurs in America, and that American guns cause almost 10 percent of the other gun violence in the world. That 90 percent of the death in this world because of gun violence is on our hands as American citizens. Choosing to do nothing is allowing it to continue.

Look at Marco Rubio, who represents Florida in the Senate. How often does he go down to Liberty City, a place where gun violence affects the community every day and they have similar homicide rates to places like Chicago? He tweets about their athletes, but how often does he head down there and say, "How can I help?" I've been down there and have met with these incredible kids and have tried to create opportunities, but it's not about us trying to be heroes, it's about us trying to empower people to save themselves from this epidemic.

I don't know what the best move is in Milwaukee, I don't know what the best move is in Las Vegas, but kids who were born and raised there and know the day-to-day problems that their community faces will be able to organize against those problems, and against the people who are perpetuating them.

We don't want students to feel like they need to experience a tragedy in order to have a voice. There are more Emma Gonzálezes and David Hoggs out there than there are people who want this to keep happening. So by organizing and inspiring people to not be afraid to speak out because of their ages and not to be afraid to be right—I think that's how we win.

HOW WE SAVE LIVES

TEN COMMONSENSE REFORMS and steps endorsed by March for Our Lives.

1. FUND GUN VIOLENCE RESEARCH.

We must provide the CDC (the Centers for Disease Control and Prevention) with dedicated funding to research gun violence as a public health issue. Even the original sponsor of the law that limits the CDC's ability to do this research, former congressman Jay Dickey, said that it was a mistake. More than one hundred medical organizations have called on Congress to restore funding.

2. ELIMINATE ABSURD RESTRICTIONS ON THE ATF.

The gun industry has operated with little meaningful oversight for far too long. ATF (the Bureau of Alcohol, Tobacco, Firearms and Explosives), the federal agency with jurisdiction to regulate the gun industry, has been operating with one hand tied behind its back—unable to even digitize records of gun sales or to require gun dealers to conduct annual inventory checks to make sure they aren't missing any guns. The ATF needs to become a modern agency, one capable of keeping receipts and efficiently regulating this massive industry.

3. INSTITUTE UNIVERSAL BACKGROUND CHECKS.

It is too easy for the wrong people to obtain a firearm. Right now, federal law requires a background check only if you purchase a gun from a licensed dealer. We must close the private sale loophole and make sure all sales undergo a background check.

4. BAN HIGH-CAPACITY MAGAZINES.

High-capacity magazines that hold more than ten rounds serve only one purpose: to allow someone to shoot as many bullets as possible in the shortest amount of time. These magazines are used in most mass shootings and need to be banned.

5. LIMIT FIRING POWER ON THE STREETS.

Weapons of war have no place in our communities. Our nation requires a comprehensive semiautomatic assault rifle ban that prohibits the future production and sale of these weapons and provides a solution for dealing with those semiautomatic assault rifles that are already owned, such as a buyback program or registration. Limiting high-powered weapons to the military has worked in other countries to eliminate the opportunity for mass shootings.

6. FUND INTERVENTION PROGRAMS.

A comprehensive approach to reducing gun violence requires not just new policies, but investment in programs that address the root causes of this violence. Federal, state, and local leaders should invest in evidence-based violence reduction strategies that engage all community stakeholders and have been proven effective.

7. INSTITUTE EXTREME RISK PROTECTION ORDERS.

There are few options available to family members concerned about an individual who is experiencing a crisis, poses a risk of harm to self or others, and owns a gun. Extreme risk protection orders provide a crucial lifesaving tool to temporarily remove a gun from a person in crisis.

8. DISARM ALL DOMESTIC ABUSERS.

While current law bans some domestic abusers from gun possession, others remain free to buy and possess the guns that are too often used to threaten and abuse. Congress needs to act to close loopholes that allow dating partner abusers, individuals convicted of stalking, and those subject to a temporary restraining order to continue possessing guns, and to make surrender of guns from prohibited abusers mandatory.

9. PASS FEDERAL LAWS SPECIFICALLY TARGETING GUN TRAFFICKING.

We know that guns move from states with weak gun laws to states with stronger laws and that illegal gun trafficking facilitates easy access to guns in impacted communities. Yet there is no federal law specifically targeting gun trafficking, making it more difficult to investigate and prosecute the criminal networks responsible for flooding communities with guns.

10. REQUIRE SAFE STORAGE AND MANDATORY THEFT REPORTING.

While many gun owners use responsible storage practices, an estimated 4.6 million children live in homes with unsecured guns, contributing to accidental deaths. There are few laws in place to ensure that guns are stored securely when not in use.

Visit marchforourlives.com/policy for more information.

IN HONOR OF THE VICTIMS OF THE SHOOTING AT MARJORY STONEMAN DOUGLAS:

Alyssa Alhadeff

Scott Beigel

Martin Duque Anguiano

Nicholas Dworet

Aaron Feis

Jaime Guttenberg

Chris Hixon

Luke Hoyer

Cara Loughran

Gina Montalto

Joaquin Oliver

Alaina Petty

Meadow Pollack

Helena Ramsay

Alex Schachter

Carmen Schentrup

Peter Wang

PHOTO INDEX